W9-BFR-890

I AM HERE

I AM HERE

Sandy Stevenson

SAMUEL WEISER, INC.

York Beach, Maine

First published in 2000 by
Samuel Weiser, Inc.
P. O. Box 612
York Beach, ME 03910-0612
www.weiserbooks.com

Library of Congress Cataloging-in-Publication Data
Stevenson, Sandy.
I am here / Sandy Stevenson.
p. cm.
ISBN 1-57863-188-2 (pbk. : alk. paper)
1. New Age movement. 2. Spiritual life—New Age movement.
I. Title.
BP605.N48 S752 2000
299—dc21 00–027027

KP
Typeset in 12.5/15 Cochin

Cover design by Sandy Stevenson
Printed in the United States of America

07 06 05 04 03 02 01 00
8 7 6 5 4 3 2 1

The paper used in this publication meets the minimum requirements of the American National Standard for Information Sciences—Permanence of Paper for Printed Library Materials Z39.48-1992 (R1997).

For a moment in eternity

Time stands still,

And what was

And will be

is now.

I Am Here

is dedicated to my mother Esmé

and to Vicky Wall

Thank You

Thank you to my family.
To my mother Esmé, words will never be enough to thank you for all you have been to me. To Talia, my beautiful loving daughter, no greater gift could I have had. To my wonderful brother Dennis—thank you for all your love and support.

Thank you to those who have touched my heart.
Brian Hasler and family, Vicky, Jono and Jenny Rogers, John Duncan, Renee, Cris, Eddie, Michael Barrymore, Robin Bee, Carole Oleson, Boy George, Peter, Sally Brown, Ann Robson, Betty McIlvenny and Gaye Symonds. There are many others.

My gratitude to those who have touched the heart of the world.
Princess Diana, Walt Disney, the Dalai Lama, Oprah Winfrey, John F. Kennedy, and Louise Hay. I have named but a few.

Thank you for the music.
To John Christian (UK), Matisha (USA), Chris James (Australia), and Sally Brown (UK), for the wonderful songs that take you "home."

Thank you Australia, my birthplace,
and England, my spiritual home.
For sharing your exquisite beauty with me.

Contents

Preface

You are going
on a special journey.
Allow the door to open
to lead your heart dancing
to a truth you have always known.
May it bring you the love you seek.

Is life just a game of chance? Is it luck that decides whether we win or lose? Is it only a dream to want to share love and understanding with everyone? We see things in life that don't make much sense. We hear of a neighbor who never harmed anyone, becoming seriously ill or getting robbed. We puzzle over what seems to be an injustice when a baby lives but a few short hours, while others are allowed their "three score years and ten."

Perhaps there are answers and we just haven't found them yet. Perhaps we think that a deeper understanding of life will be too intellectual and complicated for us. But maybe truth is simple and if it was explained this way, we could easily understand. You are about to read a story of a new way to look at life. Be open to all possibilities and let the magic change your world to one of love and joy.

For the world to change, we must first change ourselves.

You may need to let go of old beliefs. But perhaps they weren't really yours. We approach life as a young adult, weighed down with opinions and ideas we have learned from parents, books, newspapers, TV, teachers, and friends. We have acquired thoughts on every subject, from the way to behave in public to the clothes we should wear and the right food to eat. Just look at our thoughts on the weather! Gray skies are depressing; we should move to a better climate; heating is expensive; my rheumatism plays up in the cold; the sun fades the curtains; I don't like the wind. And then there are all the opinions we have about floods, droughts, brush fires, tidal waves, earthquakes, storms, lightning, and avalanches!

You have a choice, in every moment of your life.

Be willing to let go of the safety net. You don't need others to accept things first. Look and decide for yourself. Dare to lead the way. As confusion passes, you will find peace in your soul.

For peace and harmony to exist in the world,
it must first exist within us.

Let us use our precious gift of life wisely. Let us become the person we truly want to be. With more love and tolerance in our hearts, perhaps the barriers that divide neighbor from neighbor and nation from nation would disappear, allowing us to coexist in peace.

It may turn out that love is the truth we lost along the way.
Let the Golden Way unfold in your heart
and make your dreams
come true.

Important Note

Have you ever reached the end of a page and realized you didn't know what you had just read?

When reading or studying anything, it is vital to understand each word before going on. A good test of your understanding of something would be to explain it to a friend. If he or she doesn't get it, it probably isn't clear to you either.

Difficulties arise when we misunderstand words. It's not the idea you don't understand. It's the misunderstood word or words within the idea. For example, if you read, "The elderly lady had her copain to thank for her long life," you may feel you don't understand the whole idea. But it is probably the work "copain" that you don't understand. When you realize that copain means "close friend or companion," the sentence makes sense.

If you go past misunderstood words, reading can become difficult. You can lose interest in a subject and even give it up. It can also make you tired, bored, upset, headachy, or feeling stupid and overwhelmed by the whole thing. If any of these occur while reading this book, it may mean that you have gone past something you didn't fully grasp. Check this by going back to the last section you understood. Just before that point, you probably didn't understand something. Look up the words in a good dictionary. That should fix it.

Subjects such as cooking, computers, mathematics, decorating, car mechanics, carpentry, or "how to set a timer on the video" may seem complex until you understand the words. When you do, you can understand the most difficult of concepts. You may not necessarily agree with the idea, but you will at least understand it.

This makes learning easier and more enjoyable. You can learn subjects you abandoned long ago or new ones you thought were too difficult.

Unconditional Love

I love you as you are, as you seek to find your own special way to relate to the world. I honor your choices to learn in the way you feel is right for you.

I know it is important that you are the person you want to be and not someone that I or others think you "should" be. I realize that I cannot know what is best for you, although perhaps sometimes I think I do. I have not been where you have been, looking at life from your viewpoint. I do not know what you have chosen to learn, how you have chosen to learn it, with whom or in what time period. I have not walked life looking through your eyes, so how can I know what you need?

I allow you to be in the world without a thought or word of judgment from me about the deeds you undertake. I see no error in the things you say and do. In this place where I am, I see that there are many ways to perceive and experience the different aspects of our world. I allow without reservation the choices you make in each moment. I make no judgment of this, for if I would deny your right to your evolution, then I would deny that right for myself and all others.

To those who would choose a way I cannot walk, while I may decide not to add my power and my energy to this way, I will never deny you the gift of love that God has bestowed within me, for all creation. As I love you, so I shall be loved. As I sow, so shall I reap.

I allow you the universal right of free will to walk your own path, creating steps or to sit awhile if that is what is right for you. I will make no judgment that these steps are large or small, nor light or heavy, or that they lead up or down, for this is just my viewpoint. I may see you do nothing and judge it to be unworthy and yet it may be that you bring great healing, as you stand blessed by the Light of God. I cannot always see the higher picture of Divine order.

For it is the inalienable right of all life to choose their own evolution and with great love, I acknowledge your right to determine your future. In humility I bow to the realization that the way I see as best for me, does not have to mean it is also right for you. I know that you are led as I am, following the inner excitement to know your own path.

I know that the many races, religions, customs, nationalities, and beliefs within our world bring us great richness, and allow us the benefit and teachings of such diverseness. I know we each learn in our own unique way, in order to bring that love and wisdom back to the whole. I know that if there were only one way to do something, there would need only be one person.

I will love you even if you behave differently than I think you should or believe differently than I do. I understand you are truly my brother and my sister, though you may have been born in a different place and believe in another God than I.

The love I feel is for all of God's world. I know that every living thing is a part of God and I feel a love deep within for every person, animal, tree and flower, every bird, insect, river and ocean, and for all the creatures in all the world.

—Sandy Stevenson

("Unconditional Love" may be freely copied or published, providing it remains unchanged and is correctly credited.)

· CHAPTER 1 ·

Atlantis

Do you remember this day?
It was the 31st of October—14,216 years ago.

Cracks appeared down the magnificent gold and silver inner walls of the mighty temple. The surrounding temples had already collapsed, pure white columns crumbling into the waters that now lapped the edges of the steps. The mighty Healing Temple, always thought of as indestructible, was beginning to shake as the outer vibrations increased in intensity. The walls began to tilt, cracking the domed roof and showering the temple in a rainbow of glass. The beautiful amethyst crystal shattered as it hit the gold and blue marble floor.

The temple priests and priestesses stood in the center of the square below the temple as the waves began crashing further inland. They watched in disbelief, searching their minds for a reason for the chaos going on around them. It was incomprehensible. How could this be happening? They knew they had a highly advanced technology. Whole cities could be built using sound vibration alone. But it should have been safe. They had always gone to such lengths to ensure that they maintained a balance between their scientific technology and their application of the humanities. It had been ideal, with everyone coexisting in peace and harmony. Yes, there had been some problems lately, but surely not sufficient to throw the balance out this much.

They could hear the pitch of the vibration constantly increasing. It had to be connected with the intense shudder they could feel beneath their feet. They knew in their heart of hearts that it was the end. This was too intense, too devastating. With the waves mounting in intensity, it now looked as though the whole continent was going to sink.

The others who had left some months ago had foreseen it. They had said that irreparable imbalances had been created through the latest genetic experiments, causing a decline in spirituality. Many priests had said they no longer wished to be here, that disaster was inevitable. They had left for other lands, to build new pyramids and temples, and to create a new civilization as this had once been.

The ground itself began to split apart. Large chunks of land began breaking from the landmass and toppling into the ocean. Huge buildings, houses, monorail systems and bridges followed the mighty crystal healing temples into the water. As the crystals plunged through the depths, their points were smashed against sinking debris. The golden glow of their inner light was lost in the rapidly darkening waters. The crystals became more and more distressed as they attempted to stay linked to their Mother Crystal, as it, too, plummeted down through the fathoms; each of them trying to maintain their sequence of the programs that gave life to the civilizations of Earth. The giant quartz crystal, itself weighing tons, took a fairly straight path downward.

Miraculously, it landed upright and undamaged on the ocean floor of Atlan. Its program for the new millennium remained intact.

The dolphins, diving deeply, emitted high frequency sound vibrations into the path of the crystals as they tumbled and fell, to help ease their trauma and maintain a balance. The whales and dolphins had known for some time that the choices being made in Atlantis would result in disaster for their world. They were positioned in readiness, creating a huge circle of energy around the landmass. They were doing everything possible to hold things intact, in the hope that perhaps the civilization could be created again—under the water.

It took only several hours. Where once stood the mightiest and most advanced civilization ever known on Earth, there was now but a few ripples in the water. Anyone who was open to it could have sensed the magnificent Mother Crystal as it continued to emit its powerful energy. They may have felt the vortex spiraling up through the ocean waters to the sky above, an inter-dimensional energy, destined to be the source of a great future mystery, taking everything that came within its radiating sphere into another dimension.

But no one was left to feel it, or to realize that this magnificent crystal, responsible for the coordination of the entire continent, would one day confirm the existence of Atlantis.

Many years would pass, the event passing from distant memory to legend. Even the symbolic day of Halloween would fail to recall the loss of Atlantis.

· CHAPTER 2 ·

Shangri-La

6,000 years later

The family stayed behind to listen to the traveler and see what all the fuss was about. Shimara felt excited from the first moment she heard he'd arrived. The family usually left town about this time to get home to check the crops before dark. They were checking some strange patterns appearing in the fields that might be some sort of soil erosion. So far, it only affected a small area, but they were keeping a watch on it. Shimara pointed out to her husband that there was nothing they could do about this now anyway so delaying a couple more hours wouldn't matter. The children also wanted to stay, but for different reasons. They hadn't yet investigated the town's new canal. With all three eager to stay on, her husband gave in. Adrian had to admit to being more than a little curious himself. In fact, he had actually been thinking of suggesting they stay longer in order to hear the tale.

They heard rumors, of course, from people who heard it from others. But now a traveler had arrived from the province of Shangri-La. His accent showed he had truly made that long, hard journey. People were gathering now in the town square, hoping that at last some light would be shed on the stories they all heard.

The family drew closer to see the stranger better. He was tall and attractive. His fair hair was almost silver, glinting whenever the sun caught it. There was an air of peace and calm about him that brought a feeling of expectancy. Many people were now gathering, chattering excitedly among themselves. They always enjoyed these occasions, when strangers from far away parts would speak to them of the news they'd gathered on their travels. But this traveler had provoked a greater anticipation, for he was to speak first hand of something they had only heard whispers of before and had never been able to piece together.

Most of the town gathered to listen, sitting down on the blankets they placed on the hard, sandy ground of the town square. The traveler remained standing, waiting until everyone was ready.

"I have come to tell you a story about my homeland of Shangri-La. A group of us have pledged to take this story to the farthest of lands, for we feel that it may be of benefit to others." He spoke confidently and with assurance, but there was something else about him that was more difficult to define. As he spoke, his words resonated, like a long-awaited truth reaching a forgotten place deep within the soul.

"I am going to tell you of something that began some years ago. It is about a way of living we call the Golden Way.

"The town I speak of was just an average place, set in the heart of a range of mountains with peaks that shimmered in a violet haze. It was a mining town originally, but continued to expand as more people were drawn to its beautiful mountain scenery.

"The people were simple in their ways. There were still those who pottered around the old mines on the outskirts of the town, looking for a lucky find. Joe, an old miner, was one of these. He had explored these mountains most of his life. He said he didn't know what led him that day to the stream. He hadn't planned on going that way up to the ridge. It was even out of his way, but when he got to the stream, something made him decide to rest a while. He hadn't been digging or disturbing anything, but suddenly he saw the crystal, lying on the edge of the stream right in front of him. He had never seen anything like it. He'd seen crystals before, of course, often digging them up in the hills. But this one was different. It was much bigger than any he had seen. It had three points spearheading out from both ends.

"He forgot about his plans for the day and decided to take the crystal for appraisal to the assayer's office in the town. If it was valuable, he might raise enough money to pay for provisions and heating for the coming winter.

"The crystal was big, but he managed to get it into his pack. It was also quite heavy and he had to rest along the way. Whenever he stopped, he lifted back the flap of his pack and had another look at it. It certainly was a strange shape. Even the color was unusual, a sort of translucent gold that reflected an inner light.

"As he headed off to town, he told people along the way about his find. Some of them wanted to see it.

When he showed them the crystal, they all commented on how special it looked. The children, always curious to see the things he brought back from the mountains, scampered along with him as he strode to the assayer's office. He was quite excited, thinking of the possibilities it might bring.

"As chance would have it, Mac the old geologist passed by. The miner stopped to show him the treasure he'd found. The geologist held it for a while, taken by its shimmering Light. 'It certainly is beautiful,' he remarked. 'You know, some people believe that crystals have a healing power.' He handed it back to Joe. 'I suppose it's possible,' he said.

"As the miner continued on his way, he pondered over what the geologist had said. 'I wonder if they really do have a special power,' he thought. He had decided to sell it, but what if this was true? There were many people in town not as young and sprightly as they had once been. Wouldn't it be wonderful if their aches and pains could be eased? Joe was a gentle fellow, always with a kind word and a helping hand for those less fortunate. He had never been one for business anyway, usually giving away the things he found on the mountain.

"He pondered long and hard on what the geologist said and made a decision. Instead of going to the assayer's office, he went to the town hall where the people tended to gather to chat. He walked in and carefully took the crystal from his pack. 'What have you got there, Joe?' they asked. They gathered around and he showed them the crystal. 'I just came upon it,' he said, 'I found it in the same place the Daley children found those funny shaped rocks last year with the writing on them.'

"'I saw Mac Flinders on my way here. He said that he'd heard that sometimes these crystals had special healing power.' The people laughed, but they were curious and drew in to have a closer look. It was certainly a strange color, sort of opalescent with a golden glowing light. They hadn't seen anything quite like it before.

"'Well,' said the old farmer from the Kettering property, 'I'd certainly be happy if it could get rid of my backache.' An old friend of Joe's, he began to touch the crystal, running his fingers along the points. 'Well, I'll be,' he said, 'I swear my hand has gotten warmer.' The people laughed, but curiosity won them over and they began to try it for themselves. Sure enough, it happened to everyone. Some people said their hands were tingling with warmth. 'Handy for the cold weather,' said Joe's wife. That produced lots of nods and laughing. Reluctant to miss out, everyone eventually came up and touched the crystal. There was no denying that while it felt cool to touch, it certainly made their hands feel warm. Well, that had been an interesting diversion, but dusk was fast approaching and it was time for other matters. They began to wander off toward their respective homes. The crystal was dismissed, as thoughts turned to supper and the evening tasks that lay ahead.

"It was the next day that it began.

"Stories began to spread across town, first about the old washerwoman whose crippled hands made her work increasingly difficult of late. Suddenly her hands were as good as new, it was said. Then there was Billy, who limped ever since anyone could remember. He was walking straight as a rod. Still more stories were heard of ailments disappearing overnight. Then someone mentioned the crystal. It soon became clear that all the people who had suddenly become well had been at the Town Hall and touched the crystal.

"The people rushed to find Joe, to see if he still had the crystal. They told him about the people getting well. 'Well, I'll be,' he said, quite amazed, 'maybe it can heal.' They asked him if he would leave the crystal in the Town Hall, to give other people a chance to hold it. Joe happily agreed.

"Many months passed. All the people in the town became well. But it wasn't just their bodies that had healed. Somehow, their whole approach to life changed. People who never had time to spend on frivolous chatter now had a ready smile and cheerful greeting for every person they met. Arguments and disagreements became a thing of the past. Everyone seemed to be able to work things out in a friendly way. People began to share things with each other. When difficulties arose, friends and neighbors joined together to help. A good crop with surplus grain meant more for everyone, as it was shared with those less fortunate.

"Without any of the usual petty quarrels and resentment, and with problems now resolving easily, people had more time to talk to one another. This created more understanding between them. Everyday life began moving in a sort of synchronistic pattern, with all parts of it coming together in a way that made sense. The usual struggle and effort was replaced with a more productive and easy life. With love and tolerance in their hearts, everything just naturally harmonized. Slowly the town became a special place of peace and harmony, where everyone took care of each other.

"Strangers arriving in town found it most unusual. It was surprisingly easy to establish friendships. Everyone was so open and friendly, right from the beginning, that no one visiting the town wanted to leave. As the news spread of this place where joy and happiness was a part of everyday life, more people came to investigate. They were instantly made to feel welcome. Before long they would hear the story of the crystal and go to see it, to benefit from the good fortune it had shared with so many. Soon they, too, felt an inner sense of well-being. Most people stayed and had no difficulty settling into the town.

"The crystal was set on a pedestal in the Town Hall. Someone made a bronze plaque to go under it, inscribed

To bring to a close, all that may maim and harm.

As time went on, people arriving in the town didn't seem to need to go to the crystal anymore to gain the benefits of its healing. After a few weeks of living with people who were in such harmony and peace with each other, they changed as well. People began to understand that the crystal had only been a catalyst to help them change. They realized that it was the way they behaved toward each other that really changed them. Now it was up to them to continue to use their own inner strength and wisdom to maintain the harmony that had been created.

"Only an occasional visitor went to see the crystal now. They would gaze in wonder at this natural element of Earth that had instigated such a great change in the thinking of the people of Shangri-La.

It seemed so natural now to live the Golden Way that it was hard to remember how life had been before.

"The town grew into a flourishing and prosperous city. The crystal was eventually moved to the council building. The Council of Nine regularly met here with the city architects to discuss new building plans. The circular council building was typical of the new design now used in Shangri-La: pure white with gold inlay trim; flowing curved lines replacing square and rectangular patterns; and a magnificent domed roof that allowed the beauty of the sky to be seen by day or night. It was felt to be the right location for the crystal, because many of the ideas for the new city had originated from changes started with this crystal."

The traveler finished the tale of how the town had changed and began to describe it as it was now.

"Now the crystal has two plaques beneath it," he said."The second one, which we added later, simply says:

True Power is Within.

"Today, the town is a city of great beauty. We have all worked together harmoniously, sharing our ideas of what would produce an aesthetic, comfortable environment. We work with what we perceive to be a natural order of life. Most of our buildings are white with gold edging and are made of materials that do not deplete our natural resources. The curves in the designs give a pleasing quality to our landscape. We have water flowing over natural rock formations. These waterfalls are both inside and outside our homes, for we believe water to be both cleansing and calming. We have maintained large natural lakes and grassland areas among our buildings. We work with nature and have a respect for all life, so we don't harm anything that is living.

"We live a joyous life. We are honest and open with each other. It may sound unusual, but we feel a great love for one another. We also love animals and other forms of life, and consider them a part of our own lives. They are free to live naturally.

"We love the strangers who are continually arriving. As the news of our city spread, more and more people have wanted to come to live here with us. We have always welcomed them. With the extra numbers, our production levels have risen and we have become more prosperous. We all live a comfortable life, each of us working at the thing we most love. We have discovered that there is a right function for everyone, so we all have jobs that we enjoy. We feel that this is also a part of the natural order I spoke of, and it works perfectly.

"Yes, it is a beautiful city to live in, but the greatest beauty is what we've gained within us. I have tried to give you a picture of life in Shangri-La, but if I talked forever, I could never explain how wonderful it is to live in such a loving community of peace and harmony. It is a joy beyond comprehension.

"We truly believe that everyone can live like this. This is the reason the others and I began traveling, taking this story to different towns. We know that if people truly put their hearts into it, any difficulties can be overcome. It is a choice that everyone can make. You can live like this, too, if you wish.

"It was a new beginning for our town. But we lieve that it could also be the beginning of a new world.

The traveler stopped speaking.

There was silence for a few minutes, with everyone still deep in thought. It was Shimara who spoke first. "It sounds like a wonderful place. I would love to live in such a way. I suppose we all would." There was a murmur of agreement through most of the crowd. A few were shaking their heads, quite sure they could never manage to live like that.

"Would you be able to teach us this way of living?" Shimara asked.

"I would be honored to do so. If there is just one person who wants to live life in this balanced and peaceful way, it could begin to make a difference to your town."

Others began to speak up in agreement. "We would like to try," they said. "We don't know if we can do it, but we will try our best."

"I will be happy to help all I can," said the traveler. "But although I can tell you of the spiritual truths that we as a people came to understand, it is actually you who will teach yourselves. I will begin tomorrow, if you wish."

So, it came to be that the town began a new way of existence. Then another town and another, as the travelers moved on teaching the Golden Way.

· CHAPTER 3 ·

Crystal Message

A long time later

Its origin was uncertain. No one knew exactly how they had come by it in the first place. Many felt it had always been there—sitting high on the altar of the house of worship. It was rumored that a holy man had brought it over from an old ruin on the island long, long ago.

Apparently, many of the original settlers believed that the crystal had healing powers. It had always been linked to a legend of a great and wise civilization of peace that had existed in ancient times, before the ice had covered Earth. Dreamers had woven a wonderful picture of vast cities of great white temples where crystals were used for healing.

The crystal sat on the altar, unmoved for many years. Although quite a crowd attended the weekly services, few paid any attention to it these days. Every now and again, someone would give it a wash over to remove the dust that so often covered everything when the westerly gusts caught the sand.

After one special service, some of the people gathered in the nearby pavilion. They were meeting to make the final arrangements about transporting the goods they collected at the Harvest Service. Meanwhile, the children played around the lawns, making daisy chains. Some used the opportunity to climb the great yew tree when no one was looking.

One of the children went back inside the house of worship to add her daisy chain to the display of flowers that was to be taken to the old people's home. She carefully placed her little necklace of flowers around a big white flower. She stood back to look at the effect and something caught her attention. She walked over to look at the crystal, which seemed to be glowing. She glanced up at the window, to see if the sun was catching it, but there were no rays of sun visible through the stained glass. She stood gazing at the soft golden glow inside the crystal. She was drawn to it, almost mesmerized. The crystal was emitting a vibration that was somehow attuned to the child. The young girl, fascinated and dreamlike, could clearly hear words being spoken to her.

"Within our crystal structure, there is a great source of power. This power is used for the good of all mankind. In the realms of existence you came from, life is vastly different to that experienced on Earth. The people here have yet to reach a greater understanding of life that will help them to find happiness and joy. It will be your task to teach this understanding.

"You originally came from a planet far from here. You are a part of a great team who have come to Earth to bring a higher truth to this world. There are others around from your planet that are also here to help. Go to your friends and tell them of this message. You will find those who respond to it are the ones who are meant to help. If you will all gather here together, we will pass to you the knowledge we hold. This will help you complete your task. You won't need to do any more at this time, for you still have to complete your childhood. This knowledge will remain with you. Some years from now, when you have reached adulthood and the time is right, you will feel an urge to begin to speak to the people."

The child did as she was bid and brought the others. They could also hear the telepathically transmitted message, which seemed to contain a sequence of different talks. Although they didn't understand all the words, they felt in some way that they knew what it meant.

The crystal continued, "We thank you for coming. Although what has occurred here seems natural to you, many would think it strange if you were to tell them of this event. We suggest that you cast this memory to the back of your mind. There will be no need for you to think of it again for many years. One day you will know what you need to do. Meanwhile, follow the pursuits of youth and enjoy your childhood."

Over the years, the children grew strong of limb and mind, and were of a pleasing nature. However, it could be seen that even while pursuing their childhood games, there was an air of calm maturity about them.

So it came to be that as they reached adulthood, a new awareness dawned within each one. They knew the time had come that had been spoken of many years before. The nine of them gathered together and talked about the best way to reach the people. Their plans came together easily and they were in agreement with how to proceed. The city's large central park, with its peaceful, aesthetic environment of lakes, flowers, and trees, seemed an appropriate place to deliver their message.

They talked over how they would advertise the meeting. They weren't sure which one of them had thought up the title. But they all felt it reflected the truth and would attract those people who were ready to hear what they had to say. They decided to announce it as "The Future of Earth—the Golden Way."

Giving plenty of notice to allow people to arrange their busy schedules, they used this time themselves to prepare, in their own way, for the task that lay ahead. They separated to spend some time alone for inner meditation and silent contemplation of the soul.

· CHAPTER 4 ·

The Future of Earth

As told by the Crystal People

It was early evening. The balmy warm summer air caught the perfume of the flowers. The crispness of approaching autumn, with leaves just beginning to turn a soft golden color, added to the beauty of the day. It signified the time when nature begins her journey inward, seeking nourishment and strength to last through the period of silence and rest. Many people had gathered, seating themselves on the softly sloping lawns. They didn't really know what it was all about, but were interested and quite curious. It was a wonderful evening to be outdoors. The park was ideal because the children could play safely in the recreation ground. They were skipping around, happily enjoying their freedom.

The nine sat on a naturally raised part of the lawn, where everyone could easily see them. They calmly waited as people settled themselves. The people were happy to be outside on such a lovely evening. They were abuzz with chatter about what lay ahead.

As the time to begin drew near, one of the women in the group moved to the front. A strikingly beautiful young lady, with fair hair falling softly around her shoulders, she stood smiling and relaxed. It took a few minutes for the voices in the crowd to die down to a whisper. She waited patiently, seeming quite content to allow it to happen naturally.

"Hello. My name is Talia. Since we were young children, the nine of us have felt that we were to play a part in some important change that was going to happen. We didn't know how this would come about. Each of us traveled through our teenage years and gained a lot from experiencing other cultures. It was during this period, as we matured into adults, that a clearer understanding unfolded as to what we were meant to do with our lives. We realized we had a message to share about a new way of living.

"Some of our ideas will seem strange, and you will probably question our sanity," she said smiling. "Some things will conflict with what you believe. But, I wonder if all the things we believe about life are necessarily true? Or have we accepted many things because we felt that others knew best? We may have believed things we have been told by people we consider to be experts in their field. When these things are not true, we can be left with many unanswered questions about life.

"We all like stability in our lives and are not happy with things that 'rock the boat.' We like certainty and want everything to be neatly slotted in its correct place. This makes us feel comfortable and in control. When things can't easily be answered or solved, we often pretend they don't exist. We do this especially with ideas that seem strange or unusual, which we often dismiss as coming from an overactive imagination. To be able to really discover the truth, we need to keep an open mind to all sorts of possibilities. We have to be willing to listen to any new ideas.

"There is a way to establish truth. It is done by using an ability we all have. It is a spiritual ability that we often call our 'intuition' or a 'sixth sense.' It is the ability to sense something beyond what we can see. We tend to think of it more as a female thing, but men are also intuitive. It can be more developed in females, because it is acceptable in our society for women to be in touch with their feelings. In the past, men have been considered weak if they displayed their inner feelings. However, this has changed a lot. Men are now feeling more comfortable about showing their feelings.

"With our busy lives, we don't often find the time to be quiet. But it is when we are silent that we are able to hear this inner voice.

"Many cultures—from the Maya and Inca civilizations through to the more recent Hopi Indians—have prophesied that a great change was to take place on Earth. Sacred traditions have spoken of a new millennium where all life would co-exist in peace and harmony. Up until now, money and power have been the basis of operation in many societies on Earth. It is said that this will be replaced by love and compassion, where each life form will be known as equal and precious. A caring for all life will replace greed and the pursuit of material gain.

"There is already a great change occurring on Earth. I think all of us are beginning to realize that we have the power to create a world we wish to live in. We can see that giving our power of choice over to bodies such as governments, medical groups, policing organizations, religions, multinational corporations, and other authorities has not solved the problems we see in the world.

"We have recently become aware of many situations on the planet that were previously hidden from us.

Knowing about them has allowed us to make changes and choose something different. I believe we are learning to be more responsible for our own welfare.

"The power is always in the hands of the people. People are now willing to stand up and, single-handedly, make a change in the world. All the problems on Earth will be resolved when the individual, the community, the nation, or indeed humanity, take responsibility and make the decisions needed to create the world we want."

"A great need is arising for a spiritual understanding of life. A higher truth is needed to fill the emptiness we are feeling from a mainly material existence. The woman paused for a moment, a picture of serenity and beauty. The sun caught the silver in her hair.

"It is of a higher spiritual truth we wish to speak. Our message covers different areas of life and will take some months to tell. We will return here at the same time each week until we have finished. We know some of you will find many things we say a bit way out," she said smiling. "Just follow your hearts to decide if you wish to hear more.

"I am going to hand you over to Anthony. He will give the first of the messages we wish to share with you."

The woman sat down on the grass. She was obviously at ease with them all. Her voice was beautiful and easy to listen to. Her words were expressed in a way that made you feel she truly cared. Some people were sorry she had stopped. But this was quickly replaced with anticipation, as a tall man stood up to speak.

You are a spiritual Being

You have forgotten who you are

Each of you is unique

You bring a special gift to the world

You have many abilities

As Spirit, you can know anything

You are essentially good

· CHAPTER 5 ·

You

"Hello. My name is Anthony." The combination of his radiant smile, silver hair, and beautiful voice produced an instant response from the crowd. It didn't make any sense, but they felt as though they knew him. As he spoke, his words carried them to some place far away—beyond the park and the day, beyond time and space, to a world they had forgotten long ago.

"Many things happen in life that appear to make no sense. We try to gain a better understanding about life and who we are from the different philosophies and religions that offer us explanations. But, we find many of these believe their teaching is the one and only truth, so we are often discouraged from seeking truth elsewhere.

"Put aside any fears you have. Allow yourself to seek truth, wherever it may be. When you listen to the world with your heart, it opens a window to the soul. In this place, you are able to see that truth is everywhere. It flows through the rivers and the oceans. It sings through the wind in the trees and in the cry of a newly born child. It comes to our hearts in the beauty of a rainbow, as the light balances the gifts of sun and rain. It reaches us in every breath we take and whispers, 'I am here.'

"We believe there is a perfection to life, that a natural harmony and order exists in all things. We wish to give you our understanding of that order and your relationship to it. This view of life has given us the answers we sought. It has helped us gain greater inner peace and happiness, and a love and compassion for all life. We call it the Golden Way.

"Each week we will be addressing a different subject. At the beginning of each talk, we will give you seven key points that we feel will help give an overall picture of the subject. Then we will explain these points in more depth.

"You will see there is a board to our left. After each talk, we will put a parchment on it that will list the seven points we have covered that week. New people will be joining us each week and we hope this will help them understand what has been discussed in earlier talks. We have had these main points specially scripted onto smaller parchment cards. These are for you to keep as gifts. They will be available at the end of each talk. We have made them attractive, as you may wish to display them to review the points.

"The first talk is about you—who you really are.

"You are a spiritual Being,
You have forgotten who you are,
Each of you is unique,
You bring a special gift to the world,
You have many abilities,
As Spirit, you can know anything,
You are essentially good.

"When people ask you who you are, you possibly answer with your name or occupation. But this is only your current identity. You have a body, brain, mind, and an identity, but you are none of these things. You are much more than this. You are the person that controls them. We say things like 'my legs are tired,' or 'my back is aching.' Who is the 'my' we are speaking about? The answer is 'you.' If I say to you, 'Describe to me what a white dog looks like,' you will bring a picture from your mind and describe what you see. So, who is viewing that picture? Again, the answer is—you.

"You are a spiritual being—special and unique. There is no one else the same as you, anywhere. You have a special gift for the world that only you can give. You may not know what it is yet, but it will be something you enjoy doing. You may have discovered it and pushed it aside.

"Is there something you once believed in, perhaps even as a child? Did you have a goal that really excited you? Perhaps someone dismissed your idea as impractical and you let it drift away to a place of forgotten dreams. It is possible to bring your dream back to life. If it is what you are meant to do, you may be surprised at how easily your dream can become a reality. We believe that if you follow what is in your heart, events and circumstances in your life will change to help you do what you enjoy doing.

"It is easy to dismiss things you love doing as being of no commercial value. People often go out and get a 'real' job that they feel will support them financially. But you can make a living doing what you love.

Your natural enthusiasm for it attracts people. They will want the service or product you offer. You may think it has to involve lots of money. But there are also other means of support available. You can be given things, buy them cheaply, find them, win them, or exchange for them.

"It's very important to follow your passion. This means following the things in life that make your heart sing, and not sink. It doesn't have to be something glamorous. It could be anything. The key is that you will be excited about it. The ego, which is the part of you that is concerned with yourself, tells you that some jobs are more important than others. But every job is worthy and serves the community equally. Every person is an integral part of life. It all fits together in a pattern, like a giant jigsaw puzzle.

"There is a natural order to life. When you do what you love, you become a part of that order. As you begin to tune in and follow what makes your heart sing, many opportunities that you have not foreseen will open up to you. Everyone is constantly presented with choices in life. If you follow the ones that interest or excite you, your life will become wonderfully rewarding. You could also feel excited by the ego's desire for wealth, sensation, or fame. So you will need to be able to tell the difference between the two.

"You are already a wonderful spiritual being with many special qualities. Although many people are confident about their ability to handle life, there are also many who underestimate themselves. You may see people doing things you think are clever and believe that this makes them better than you. You might think you're not very intelligent because society tells us that intelligent people have clever jobs and make a lot of money. But intelligence is really just common sense. It is the ability to handle life. Whether you are a parent bringing up several children or a doctor performing surgery, immense talent and ability is required to achieve this. The parent or the doctor may consider they are not clever enough to do the other person's job. However, each of us has different gifts, comparing yourself with other people doesn't give a true picture.

"We are here on Earth to learn greater wisdom. We are working on gaining new abilities to assist us to become even more wise and loving. Some of the spiritual qualities we may be trying to learn are patience, humility, integrity, wisdom, power, confidence, hope, compassion, truth, strength, comfort, gentleness, patience, thoughtfulness, determination, kindness, clarity, balance, harmony, respect, humor, generosity, faith, peace, forgiveness, trust, understanding, grace, laughter, dedication, playfulness, devotion, purity, commitment, Divine will, credibility, compassion and tolerance. We mostly gain these bit by bit as we experience life.

"There is so much to the picture of life. Some of you will have already come across the ideas we speak of. To others, these ideas will be new and strange. We understand that you will want to discuss what we have said with your friends. This will help. But, please understand that in the beginning it can be confusing. It may take some weeks of our talks before you start to get an overall picture. Eventually it will become clear.

For those of you who would like to hear more, we will be here at the same time next week."

The people slowly wandered away, pondering over what they had heard. Some were shaking their heads, muttering that it was all ridiculous and too much to take in. Some felt it was a bit frightening. Some people spoke quietly in reverence, believing that they were being given a special gift, perhaps even a real opportunity to make things different. "Maybe it is a blessing to help us all live a better life," they said. Many people were in deep discussion as they walked off into the dark toward their homes. Some walked along in silence, looking at the bright stars sprinkled across the deep navy sky. They seemed to whisper softly through the darkness, "The answers will lead you to joy untold."

Discussions about the whole event raged all week long. Among families and friends, in homes and in work places, arguments began and ended. Some people almost came to blows. It appeared to be the main topic of conversation. Judging by the amount of time spent discussing it, there could have been little else done that week. New issues were raised about the morality and values involved, and even more arguments were put forth.

As the time drew near, most people decided to return. The news had spread and many people who had not been present the previous week could not avoid hearing about it. In the end, their curiosity got the better of them and they also went along.

People rested on the grass in the early evening warmth. Some were still skeptical. Some were eager for the proceedings to start. Others pretended they had nothing better to do. But many were determined to take any opportunity to improve their lot.

By the time the nine arrived, quite a crowd had gathered.

Life

You chose to come to Earth

You have probably been here before

You chose your parents

You were aware of your life circum-

stances

You are here to learn

You choose your learning

You keep coming back until you

have learned it all

· Chapter 6 ·

Life

Talia, the lady who had first spoken to them, stood up to speak. This time her fair hair was swept back from her face, showing her lovely gray-green eyes. They felt very much at ease with her, much the same as you would with a close friend. You had the impression she would never be too busy to listen, and would advise with wisdom and understanding, despite the fact she was obviously the youngest of the group. They waited expectantly.

"I see we have more people this week. For those of you who were not here last week, we spoke about who we 'really' are. Not the identity people see themselves as, but the real us—as spiritual beings. Perhaps after we finish this evening, some people who were present last week could pass on details of that talk to you. It won't be possible for us to go back over the things we have previously covered, so if you bring any new people in the weeks to come, please share with them as much detail of the previous talks as possible.

"We mentioned last week that our talks include seven key points. The board over there will show all the points that have been covered. We also have free cards listing these points, available at the end of each talk.

"This week we hope to give you further insight into last week's subject. I am going to talk about the purpose of life.

"You chose to come to Earth,
You have probably been here before,
You chose your parents,
You were aware of your life circumstances,
You are here to learn,
You choose your learning,
You keep coming back until you have learned it all.

"You could think of Earth as a school that offers teaching, from kindergarten to university level. You are given opportunities to learn through the ordinary, everyday things that happen in your life. You have come here to learn to be a wiser, more loving and tolerant person. You achieve this by personally experiencing different circumstances designed to help you learn. For example, if you lost a pet or had something stolen, wouldn't you be better able to comfort someone with a similar loss?

"You can take as long as you like to learn something. You all learn in your own way, at your own pace. Sometimes things happen many times before you grasp the lesson it teaches. Sometimes you'll learn very quickly. You can learn from everyone, be it a child, adult, friend or enemy.

"You have lived many lives. Each time, you had a new body and a new identity. You have been male and female. You have had different nationalities, religions, education, languages, and customs. You learn from experiencing the many different conditions in life. Whether king or peasant, rich or poor, master or servant, educated or not, Catholic or Hindu, a priest or a thief, they are all equal ways to learn.

"To achieve real wisdom, life needs to be seen from different angles. Therefore, many roles need to be experienced. A king may learn wisdom by governing others, a rich man may learn happiness from giving, and a peasant may find joy in a simple life. A thief may rise above greed, a parent may learn love from a child, and a priest may learn of faith. A waitress may wish to learn the value of serving others, and a bullied child may discover inner strength. But these are just examples. There is no set learning for any particular role. It could be that the waitress is supposed to learn patience, and the king is to learn to serve others. We are usually offered many different lessons in each life.

"You might say, 'But, I don't remember being anyone else before.' There is a reason why people don't remember past lives. Let us say you had chosen to be 'poor' in this life, in order to experience life from the eyes of a poor person. Would you really learn what this was like if you remembered that you had chosen to be poor? The answer is that you would have to truly believe yourself to be poor, in order to fully experience it.

"All of you plan the major events in your lives. If this were not done, it would very much be a hit and miss affair. Then it could take a very long time to achieve all the qualities you seek.

"You live many lifetimes, each time gaining more wisdom and understanding. Your purpose is to learn the highest form of love. This is called unconditional love. It is the ability to love everyone, everywhere, without attaching any conditions to that love. You may wonder how you could love a stranger. But you can. And not only a stranger, but a thief or murderer, as well. You may think this is impossible. Although it can be difficult, many people have achieved it. We hear of people who have forgiven someone who has caused them great suffering, such as the death of a child.

There is another type of love called conditional love. This is when we decide we can only love someone if they behave as we think they should, or if they are the same as us—perhaps the same religion or nationality. This happens more often than we realize. Conditional love occurs when we have expectations of people that they fail to live up to and we react to this by withholding our love.

"Maybe we expect a partner to make an effort to dress for a formal event and he or she arrives in casual clothes. A shopkeeper may not be friendly and we show our displeasure. A friend may have promised to phone us but he or she forgets. Perhaps we gave someone a nice gift, but didn't receive one in return. Maybe we thought a friend could have helped us more. If we loved someone less because of his or her actions, that is conditional love. In these cases, what we are saying is, I will only love you if you do what I think you should. I will love you when you meet my conditions.

"If the level of our love does not alter in these instances, even a little, this is very special. This shows us we are much closer to attaining our goal. Remember we are speaking of love in its spiritual sense, which is the ability to love all people and all life.

"We will be speaking more later on the subject of love.

"As we grow more wise, we begin to understand how we share life with everyone and everything. Finally, we attain the ability to love all life unconditionally. Having reached that, we are then able to move on to a higher level of learning.

"This ends today's talk. We will see you here next week. We will be talking about a precious gift of life—the birth of a child."

Birth

Each child is special and brings its own gift to the world

The parents and baby have chosen each other

A baby has lived before as both male and female

The parents and child may have been together before

The family circumstances are known prior to birth

The baby has chosen the best situation for its learning

The baby has six weeks to change its mind and leave

· Chapter 7 ·

Birth

The conversations around the park were mostly about last week's talk. The idea of having lived before was still a bit hard to grasp. People were handling this idea by making up jokes about their past lives. They noticed that a stage had been set up for this week and were joking about what play was coming on. They were having lots of fun deciding which famous past-life person they might have each been.

Then the thought was proposed that they couldn't all have been famous. "There must have been many times when we were poor, maybe even starving," suggested one lady. "We might have been slaves?" "Or even a school teacher," added another man. "Just think, I might have done this before! Will I never learn?" he groaned. That produced a lot of laughter from the crowd.

Just then, Anthony came forward. "Hello everyone," he said, laughing with them, "It's good to see you all in such high spirits. Isn't it interesting that we use *high spirits* to mean joy? For those who were not here when I spoke at our first meeting, my name is Anthony."

The new people warmed to him instantly. Again, his voice touched upon some special memory, held somewhere just beyond reach.

He continued, "We now have a platform to allow everyone to be able to see clearly. I realize the reason for it being here is not as exciting as a play with wonderful historical characters in it," he said smiling. The people began laughing, realizing that the group had overheard their jokes.

"We believe that our discussion this week is another link in the overall understanding of who you are and the purpose of your life here. This week I want to speak about something very special—the birth of a baby.

"Each child is special and brings its own gift to the world,
The parents and baby have chosen each other,
A baby has lived before as both male and female,
The parents and child may have been together before,
The family circumstances are known prior to birth,
The baby has chosen the best situation for its learning,
The baby has 6 weeks to change its mind and leave.

"We each come to Earth to learn. The person, the Spiritual Being, wants to become wiser through the experiences it can have in a physical world. It knows it will encounter limitations in everyday life, and hopes to gain strength and wisdom by rising above them.

"The baby has chosen its parents. Prior to being born, it is aware of all the circumstances that relate to that family. This means it knows beforehand whether it will be male or female, or if it will have brothers or sisters. It understands the parents' relationship and financial status, as well as their customs, religion, and nationality. It knows of its grandparents. It knows whether it will experience tough conditions as a child, and whether it will be loved, abused, adopted, or abandoned. You may think this is ridiculous—why would anyone wish to be adopted or abused? But many roles are chosen to attain growth, strength, and wisdom.

"The agreement concerning the children is made with all members of the family. So everyone gets together to work this out. This is done even before the birth of the parents. It is quite usual for the baby and parents to have been together in a previous life. In fact, you have often been together with some or even all of your current family and friends. However, the previous relationship you had was probably different. Many roles are swapped. For example, your current mother may have been your father or a distant relation. Your sister or brother may have been a friend, acquaintance, or your child. This doesn't mean that you have relationships with only the same few people. Remember, you live many lifetimes.

"So, this Being is now in a new baby body. After the freedom of the Spirit world, life is quite restrictive. The human body only has five senses—sight, hearing, smell, touch, and taste. Spirit has many senses, such as being able to see with a 360-degree view. Being in a physical body is also limiting in that it is very sensitive to injury and temperature. It also has to have food, air, warmth, and water to survive. There are other forms of restrictions for the Being as well. The nationality, social class, culture, and religion that have been chosen for the lifetime may be very restrictive.

"As we said, the baby has made certain agreements with the parents. There is a period of six weeks when the baby may check to see that the life circumstances are still as agreed. If it appears that something has changed that will prevent the learning needed, the baby can leave. This is one of the causes of crib death.

"Many children retain a conscious awareness of their previous life. If we listen, they quite often say things that support this. A direct question to a 3-year-old, such as 'Where were you before you came to Mummy?' often produces an amazing answer. Many young children volunteer this information. However, it is usually ignored as being childish imagination and received with comments such as, 'Don't be silly, you can't have been up in the stars.' Providing it is made safe for them to tell the truth, they will.

"Young children have a great ability to love unconditionally. They also need lots of love, as we all do," he said smiling. "They have a wonderful capacity to live in each moment for the pleasure of that moment. We can learn a great deal from observing our children. They are far more wise than people assume. Remember that your children have probably come to you from a previous life. They may have been married with three children or have been a 70-year-old mathematics professor! They may also have been from any religion, nationality, or social class and even of the opposite sex. That idea may require a little adjusting to," he said laughing.

"That completes the talk for this week. I hope this helps you to understand that you have all chosen to be with the family you have." Anthony said, "I know it may sometimes seem that there is a war going on between family members. But you may discover one day that those closest to you are often your greatest teachers. Next week we will be talking about death. We intend to give a different and very positive view of the subject."

Death

You never die

You are immortal and infinite

Your body is an overcoat you use for
a lifetime

It is you who keeps the body alive

When your body dies, you leave it

Death is only a change of reality

Death occurs to give you opportunities
for growth

· CHAPTER 8 ·

Death

This time a new person from the group stood up. He was shorter, with dark hair and had a much stockier build than Anthony. He appeared to be younger, but his eyes told of a maturity far beyond his years. There was a depth to them that spoke of an overcoming of something. It was difficult to guess what that had been. Perhaps he had experienced great pain or suffering in his life.

"Welcome everyone. My name is Mark. We see that your numbers are growing. We must be doing something right! Or perhaps there is a shortage of any other entertainment this evening." The people appreciated the joke. They knew what was about to be discussed and were a little apprehensive.

"I will just mention, for the new people here, that each week we cover a different subject about life. We begin with seven main points that we feel will give you an overall view of the subject. Then we cover them in more detail. The key points are written on that board over to my left. We also have cards with these points listed, available free at the end of each talk.

"Our purpose in being here is to give you another viewpoint on life. Many of the things we say will seem strange; as I am sure you have already been told." The people laughed. "We ask you to bear with us until you have heard the whole picture we offer. We do not wish to impose our will in any way. It is your choice to accept what we say or not.

"We have spoken about birth and life. Now we will talk about how we see the subject of death.

"You never die,
You are immortal and infinite,
Your body is an overcoat you use for a lifetime,
It is you who keeps the body alive,
When your body dies, you leave it,
Death is only a change of reality,
Death occurs to give you opportunities for growth.

"Death is simply a change from your human form to your spiritual form. When your physical body dies, you leave it. You then return to your true state as a spiritual being. Your body is made from matter, so it returns to its natural state. It goes back to the earth, being cremated or buried. You also return to your natural state, which is in the realm of the Spirit World. You are most definitely alive. In fact, you never die. You cannot. You are eternal and immortal.

"Although your physical body is gone, you have another body, a *spiritual* one. You have always had this throughout your life, but it cannot be seen. It is quite similar in appearance to your physical body. The reason it can't be seen with the human eye is because it is more *see through*, or transparent. This body stays with you when you *die*.

"As you *die*, you may experience a tunnel or stream of light. You might have heard this mentioned by people who have had what they call a near death experience. This tunnel feels safe, which encourages you to proceed along it. You are met by someone you know and love, often a departed family member, an angel, or a guide. This helps you feel comfortable.

"Although consciously you may not know that you are about to die, you always know this on a spiritual level. The moment of death, and the circumstances that surround it, are usually prearranged before you are born. Suicide, however, is not normally prearranged. Nor is it something to be condemned or judged. Everything in life is a choice. People who commit suicide may later see this as a waste of a lot of planning, but no one else is going to judge it. When people commit suicide, it can happen that they break agreements made with others for this lifetime. In this case, the people affected will have new plans arranged for them by their guides.

"After you leave the physical world, you rest and adjust in a place called the Astral Plane. This place looks a lot like the world you just left behind. Because of this, it feels comfortable and helps ease the changeover. Here you adjust to the idea that *you* are still alive.

"Because this place looks so similar to where they have been, some people don't realize for a while that they have died. This is the explanation for ghosts. Ghosts are people who have died, but who have not yet accepted that they are dead. There is a tendency for ghosts to stay around familiar places. When people see a ghost, it is the person's spiritual body they are seeing. When people eventually realize they have died, they move on to a higher level. We will be explaining this more fully next week.

"If you think you may have ghosts in your home, you can help them. Gently explain to them that although the physical body has died, they are still alive. I have suggested that this is done gently because it can be a bit of a shock to realize that you have *died!* Let the person know that it is time to move on and that everything will be all right. Tell the person there are people who are waiting to help. The person will be fine. Everyone has guides who will help him or her move on, whenever he or she is ready to go. These guides are often people that the person was close to during life that have now passed on. Our guides always permit us to do things in our own time. They would never interfere, for instance, by telling someone that his or her body had died. That would take away the person's right of choice.

"A person can stay as long as he or she likes in the Astral Plane. If the death was sudden, or the person had strong beliefs about what happened at death, it can take longer to adjust. For example, if a person believed that dying means he or she won't exist anymore, it may take a while to get used to the truth. If someone already has an understanding of spiritual matters before death, the length of time spent in the Astral Plane can be very short.

"The amount of time we stay in this plane does not really matter, because time is different in the spirit world. From a human point of view, we could say that it may be more beneficial that the person gets on with his or her next life and the learning that can be obtained from it. However, I want to take this opportunity to express a different viewpoint on what is beneficial. The more we understand life from a spiritual perspective, the more we begin to see a perfection to the order of things throughout life and death that we couldn't see before. If the person needs to adjust to the idea of having died, then it would be more beneficial that he or she be permitted to take as long as is necessary to make this adjustment.

"The family member or guide who meets the person at the point of death stays close by. The guide quietly allows the person to readjust to the new circumstances and will then offer guidance if it is needed.

"That concludes this week's talk. I hope this has been of some help for any of you who may have concerns about dying. We look forward to seeing you here again next week."

In Between Lives

After death, you go to a higher level of existence

Here you are helped by friends and guides

You look at the circumstances and lessons of your life

You look at this from a higher level of understanding

You are the only reviewer and the only judge

You see what was learned and what you still need to learn

Then you plan out a new lifetime for further learning

· Chapter 9 ·

In Between Lives

"Hello. My name is Diana."

They warmed to her immediately. Fair hair softly framed her exquisite face and twinkling blue eyes. There was a lightness and playfulness about her. You could tell she would be lots of fun to be with. In fact, they often saw her joking with Anthony, as he tried to arrange the scroll cards in neat stacks on the stage. She kept toppling them over, just as he had gotten them so precisely right. She would run off laughing. He tried to look serious, but inevitably he would laugh and start again. Perhaps it was her way of showing him that they didn't need to be so precisely arranged.

"We are happy to see so many people here this week. Those of you who are newly arrived have probably heard about some things we have been discussing. Please forgive us if something we say doesn't make sense, but each talk follows on from the last. If you find anything confusing, perhaps you would like to ask people who have been here before to help clear it up for you. They will all have a complete understanding of everything we have covered so far." The people laughed, enjoying the joke.

"We have talked of birth and death. Now we will talk about the time in between death and birth.

> *"After death, you go to a higher level of existence,*
> *Here you are helped by friends and guides,*
> *You look at the circumstances and lessons of your life,*
> *You look at this from a higher level of understanding,*
> *You are the only reviewer and the only judge,*
> *You see what was learned and what you still need to learn,*
> *Then you plan out a new lifetime for further learning.*

"After your body dies, you go to a higher level of life. It is a level of spirit. As we said last week, this place looks similar to your normal surroundings. This helps you make the adjustment. It is a pleasant place. Before long, you adjust to the idea that you are still alive and it was only your body that died. Then you are able to move on to an even higher level.

"Now you begin to look over the life you have just left. You see how you handled everything. You look at the lessons involved in all the experiences you had. You see which lessons you learned and which you didn't.

"The reason you look back over your life is not to make judgments of whether you were right or wrong. You are looking at your life now from your spiritual viewpoint of a desire to learn. It is different from the perspective you had while you were living your life.

"There are many different things to see. For example, you would look at whether you were positive and loving. Or whether you allowed negative thoughts and judgments to dominate your life. You would see if your actions brought joy and happiness to others or whether you hurt anyone unjustly. You see whether you forgave people who hurt you, or if you could have been more tolerant.

"When you have finished, you can see whether you gained what you had hoped to during your lifetime.

"Now you begin to plan your next life. Remember you are coming to Earth to learn. You are going to plan experiences that will give you the best opportunities to learn. You hope to become more wise by overcoming the obstacles that you set for yourself. You therefore go to a lot of trouble in the planning stage. If you do need any help with this, there are people available to help you. These are called guides. If, for example, you are having any difficulty seeing exactly what type of situations will give you the best chances to learn, your guides may assist with some possible ideas.

"Let us say that you wish to learn how to be a better father. You have planned to have several children to help you with this. Your guides may suggest that you also have a lot of brothers and sisters to help you begin learning about good parenting as a child. They may also think it might be beneficial for you to spend some time working in a children's home. It could even be suggested that you arrange with those people who are to be your parents, that you are the eldest child and that your father dies at an early age. This would allow you the opportunity to become a father quite early on. However, these would only be offered as suggestions. It will be you who choose the situations that will occur in your life.

"You plan out all the major parts of your life. You would plan your family, nationality, education, and financial status. You would decide your main obstacles, your work, your relationships, and the number of children you will have. Your plans are made with those people who will be your family members, children, close friends, and so on. You have often been with many of these people before, in other lifetimes. Because of this, love already exists prior to you meeting them. This often accounts for the instant feeling of love you have with some people.

"It will also happen that you have people in your life that you did not get on well with in a previous life. This can account for instant feelings of dislike. However, these people are there for a reason. Nothing is ever accidental. Maybe, when looking from a spiritual viewpoint, you realized that a certain person had not harmed you as previously thought, but had been helping you learn something. Believing they had harmed you, you consequently had treated them quite badly. So you have chosen to meet them again in your current life, to help fix the upset you created at the time. Or it may be that as you now see they were helping you, you want to return the favor and help them this time.

"You may feel that your life is predestined. To some degree it is, but it is you who arranges it. You are trying to give yourself the best chance for spiritual growth. You can change any of it at any time. You always have free will and choice.

"After you are born, you won't remember the plans you made. You use your intuition to guide you to what will best help you. Some of you may call this a *gut feeling*, or *following your heart*.

"There are also signs given in your life that point you in the right direction. For example, let's say you want to be a nurse. You will be helped to discover this. Perhaps a situation arises where you have to look after someone who is ill. While you are doing this, you realize you like it. Perhaps you meet someone who tells you about the wonderful care they had from the nurses while in hospital. You could be reading a magazine and find an article of interest about a new system of patient care. You may find you are interested in watching hospital movies on television. You get lots of signs. Watch for the things that you find interesting.

"There are three areas that direct your behavior. These are mind, ego, and intuition. If you want to be in the best place to learn all you chose to learn in your life, you need to follow your intuition. But sometimes you listen to your mind or ego. The mind gives you reasons and excuses. The ego worries about what others think of you, or what you think of yourself.

"Here's an idea of how these three areas work. You are invited to an outdoor fancy dress party. You are excited about going as a fairy princess. The feeling of excitement is your intuitive guidance. But your ego may tell you that people will think you look silly. Your mind may think that a white dress is not practical for an outdoor event.

"When you choose to ignore your intuition, you may alter a part of your plan. For example, let's say that when you planned your life, you arranged to meet up with a particular person. This is meant to happen when you both go to work for the same company. Both of you intend to gain some experience in this company and then leave to set up a design company together. This does not mean that every job we do is preplanned. However, sometimes things need to be this specific.

"Let's imagine that you have now reached that point in your life. You have decided to work as a professional designer. This is something you enjoy and are qualified to do. You have handed in your notice at your current job. You are going to apply for a job with a well-known design firm. Then the company you are about to leave suddenly offers you a higher salary if you stay on. You don't want to stay, but there is a certain amount of fear involved in the step you are about to take. The mind comes in with its usual thoughts. 'What if it doesn't work out?' 'What if I don't get the other job?' or, 'I may be on a lower salary and won't be able to pay off the house.'

"Despite a sinking feeling in your heart, you agree to stay on. But in doing so, you have changed your plan. In addition, you have also broken the agreement you made with the other person.

"Sometimes, these things turn out all right. You may get another opportunity to meet up. Or, maybe a week later, you feel so bad about your decision, that you decide to leave the company after all. Even though it happens later than planned, it may work out. You managed to catch it before anything changed. What could happen when you didn't show up, is that the person made some other arrangements.

"We all get help with this type of situation. I would like to explain how this happens. Just as we made agreements with our family members, before birth, we also made arrangements with guides. These are people who will help guide us to the learning we want. Some of these will be people you meet in your life. But others will be people who help us from a spiritual level. They aren't living in a physical body. You can relax," she said laughing, "You don't suddenly hear a voice in your head. They just help make the signs around you a little clearer.

"We have a choice in the decisions we make. You may say, 'But what about people who are afraid, or need security, or who lack confidence in themselves? They don't have a choice.' But is this true? We can choose whether or not we let that fear dictate our lives. We can also try to overcome our fears or gain confidence. If we really want to, we can find a way. It doesn't have to cost money. There are library books, friends, family, free talks, and free counseling available.

"Trusting your inner guidance will definitely bring you an easier and more enjoyable life.

"We will be talking more about the choices you have in life a little later. We will see you all next week. Thank you."

Illness

You are capable of healing yourself

You are the source of your own illness

The way you think affects your health

Life is a mirror that reflects our thoughts back to us

Negative thoughts can create illness

Letting go of negative thoughts can make you well again

Positive thoughts create a well and happy person

· Chapter 10 ·

Illness

The people sat waiting expectantly. They hadn't been told what this week's talk was about and they were curious. With their numbers still growing each week, many people were coming earlier to get a place closer to the stage. The talks were never very long. A lot of people felt this was just as well. There were quite enough ideas for them to grasp as it was.

These summer evenings were so pleasant that many people had taken to staying on to chat after the talks had finished. It was helpful to discuss what had been said. Many people were there alone and didn't feel they understood enough yet to share it with their families. Those who were more familiar with the ideas being given in the talks were helping others who were still trying to work it out.

The man who came forward to speak this afternoon was quite tall. He had a beautiful face, with that same male and female quality they had seen in Anthony. It was difficult to pinpoint his age. There were some lines on his face, but they didn't fit with the overall impression one had of agelessness. They also felt a sense of compassion in him, as if he somehow understood how difficult life can be at times.

"Hello. My name is Michael. I am going to talk about illness. You may find this subject the hardest of all to accept. Then again, you may feel the same thing applies to all our talks," he said laughing. "Most people tend to have some very definite views about illness. Probably most of us feel that getting sick is just bad luck—something that is beyond our control. We are going to suggest a possible alternative."

His broad smile relaxed them somewhat, although they had a feeling they may not stay that way for long. Some people began to mentally prepare for the discussions and possible arguments that might follow during the coming week. He stood quietly, smiling, aware of their concerns. He spoke again, "Remember this is only our view of things. You may decide that what we say is fiction, or the result of a vivid imagination on our part. Whatever you believe is all right with us. It is important we each make up our own minds. In this way, we become masters of our life.

"You are capable of healing yourself,
You are the source of your own illness,
The way you think affects your health,
Life is a mirror that reflects our thoughts back to us,
Negative thoughts can create illness,
Letting go of negative thoughts can make you well again,
Positive thoughts create a well and happy person.

"Let's begin with an exercise. Get a picture in your mind of a large, yellow lemon. Good. Cut it in half. Now take a big bite into the lemon. Do you feel a reaction—

perhaps an increase in saliva in your mouth, or a sour taste? What happens is that your mind associates, or connects, biting into a lemon with the sensation you felt in your mouth. It makes this connection from previous experiences that are recorded in your mind. You don't have to actually eat the lemon. Just the thought of doing so produces a physical reaction in your body. So you see your thoughts can affect your physical body.

"You may recall a time in your life when you made yourself ill. You might have been avoiding something you didn't want to do, such as going to school. We can all deliberately make ourselves ill. We start off pretending to feel ill and then it really happens. We have a great ability to create things with our thoughts.

"We can also make ourselves ill accidentally, by thinking in a negative way. We will be talking more fully next week about our thoughts, but negative thoughts are those where we express failure, fear, lack of confidence, despair, criticism, or judgment. These are different types of negative thoughts. For example, 'It's no use trying, I never win,' shows we have despaired or given up. 'He is stupid,' is a criticism or a judgment. 'What would people say,' means we may be allowing other people to decide what we do. 'You may have an accident' would be expressing fear.

"Different illnesses can come from different types of negative thoughts. I will give you some examples. Hip problems can come from a fear of going forward in life, or from thinking that there is nothing worthwhile ahead of you. There are different types of cancer and the causes are varied. Cancer can result from a deep hurt, a long-standing resentment, a deep secret, grief eating away at the self; carrying hatred, or a 'what's the use' attitude. Arthritis can come from being critical, resentful or feeling unloved. Lower back problems can be a fear of money or a lack of financial support.

"High blood pressure sometimes comes from a long-standing unsolved emotional problem. Low blood pressure could be caused from being unloved as a child or having the attitude of 'It's no use, it won't work anyway.' Bowel problems can come from a fear of releasing old ideas. Knee problems can show a stubborn ego or pride or being inflexible. Problems with the mouth can show a closed mind, set opinions or an incapacity to take in new ideas. Neck troubles can be a stubbornness and a refusal to see the other side. Sprains can come through anger and resistance or not wanting to move in a certain direction in life. Stuttering may be from feeling insecure, a lack of self-expression or not being allowed to cry. Teeth problems may be caused from a long-standing indecisiveness or the inability to break down ideas for analysis and decisions. Thyroid trouble can be from an attitude of, 'I never get what I want, when is it going to be my turn?'

"We are all trying to learn to be more positive and loving. Negative thoughts make it difficult to achieve this. So, if we are being negative, we need to find this out. To help us, life acts like a reflection in a mirror. It gives us a message. It will show us other people doing the same things that we do. If we believe in failure, we will see others fail. If we are impatient, we will meet impatient people. Hopefully, we then realize that we are doing it and we stop.

"In the beginning, you might only occasionally see someone behave this way. But if you don't stop doing it, it happens around you more often. All the time the lesson draws closer to you. It may start with a stranger, but after a while it will be your friends and partners who display the same behavior as you.

"Let's look at an example. Perhaps you are 'too loving.' This sort of behavior can make people feel smothered or trapped. Life's mirror might show you neighbors who never let their children out of sight, stifling the children with overprotective love. You are seeing this to help you look at your own behavior. If you don't stop being too loving, you will begin to see more people act this way. If it remains unhandled, then someone close to you may start to smother you. Alternately, it may be that you are not loving enough, in which case, people will be unloving toward you. Being too loving or not loving are both negative behaviors.

"If you keep seeing people behave a particular way, check to see if you ever do the same thing. The behavior you see in others will always be more exaggerated than yours. This helps you to see it more easily. Interestingly, when you stop doing it, you will no longer see anyone else do it. The people who were doing it either stop, or they move out of your life, or you just don't notice it anymore.

"If you still fail to realize you are being negative, the messages begin to change. The signs are no longer external signs. They also become internal. Now they start to react on your body. Now it becomes a pain, illness, or disease. It can start in a mild way, such as a twinge, but if ignored, can gradually increase to severe pain or long-term illness.

"For example, the heart represents love. So, negative thoughts concerning love can cause heart problems.

If we don't stop these thoughts, it can lead to a more serious heart condition, perhaps even death. Therefore, thoughts are very important.

"You can become ill from taking or coming in contact with something poisonous. Many allergies that people are experiencing come from overloading the body with chemicals in food, medicines, furnishings, and life style. But some people are more likely than others to become ill in this way. Thinking in a negative way weakens your resistance to illness. This is why not everyone gets ill when subjected to identical conditions.

"There are other reasons why people become ill. This next explanation may be a little hard to accept. It is possible you have chosen to have a particular illness or condition. Your immediate response may be, 'Why would I ever do that?' Well, it has to do with what you came here to learn. Perhaps, when you reviewed your previous life, you saw that you always had difficulty accepting help from people. So now you have put yourself in a position where you will be forced to accept help. Or you may have seen that you lacked compassion for sick people, and felt it may help if you experience what it is like to be ill.

"Maybe you are helping someone else learn something. For example, have you ever seen a family grow more loving and patient through caring for a sick or disabled child or relative? This type of situation may have been arranged by all concerned when planning out the lifetime.

"The ideas I've shared today are probably quite different from how you have thought about illness in the past. I know it may not be easy to look at such a different view. But we only ask that you consider the possibility. With this knowledge, you may find that you are more able to help yourself and others get well.

"Thank you for listening. We greatly appreciate you giving us your time. As usual, free cards showing the seven key points are available on the right side of the stage.

"Next week's talk will cover how our thoughts affect the way we see the world. I think you will find it interesting. Enjoy your evening."

Thoughts

Your thoughts create the way you see the world

Changing your thoughts will change your life

Positive thoughts can change the world

Negative thoughts create disorder and illness

Thoughts influence other people

Thinking positively is natural

Positive thoughts make a happy life

· CHAPTER 11 ·

Thoughts

Despite the forecast for rain, it had not seemed to deter anyone. The lawns were covered with the usual number of people. The sky was overcast. There was murmuring through the crowd about whether they should have brought their umbrellas. Someone said it was a pity they couldn't move to an indoor shelter. Someone else mentioned that it would have to be pretty big; had they looked lately at just how many people were here? Most of them were pretty sure they would be soaked by the time they got home. They were a bit agitated by these thoughts, but not enough to leave. They didn't want to miss anything important. It was nearly time to start. The voices of the crowd began to quiet to soft whispers.

Devora, one of the nine who had not spoken before, moved to the front of the platform. There was an air of peace and serenity surrounding her. She didn't speak. She just stood quietly, smiling and looking at them. They could feel that this gentle and beautiful lady had somehow moved beyond a world that criticized and judged. She accepted and loved them, just as they were. The love that came from her reached into their hearts, giving them a feeling of coming home. The minutes went by. As they looked at her, their agitation disappeared. Slowly, everyone began to relax, surprised at how peaceful they felt.

As she stood there, the sky began to clear. The darker clouds vanished and in minutes were replaced with a beautiful aqua-blue haze that covered the horizon. There were soft tinges of pink in the sky as dusk foretold a beautiful sunset. As the last rain-carrying clouds passed by, she began to speak. Her words danced across the distance, and as the sun spilled over them, the people felt they were being given a message that went far beyond the words they could hear.

"Our subject this week is about the power of thought," she said smiling.

"Your thoughts create the way you see the world,
Changing your thoughts will change your life,
Positive thoughts can change the world,
Negative thoughts create disorder and illness,
Thoughts influence other people,
Thinking positively is natural,
Positive thoughts make a happy life.

"Your thoughts play an important part in your life. They are the way you choose to look at the world. They influence what you experience. For example, you may see rain as preventing you from going outdoors. That thought may make you feel discontented. However, if you chose to view rain as a beautiful gift that is essential for growth, this positive viewpoint might make you feel grateful and happy when it rains.

"Positive thoughts enhance your life and the lives of the people around you. When you maintain a positive outlook about all the things you see and experience in life, you align with what we call Divine Order. It is the natural flow of order that exists in the world. Living 'in the flow,' as they say, creates a calm and peaceful life, filled with happiness and joy. Positive thinking creates a healthy mind and body.

"Negative thoughts and behavior are harmful. They produce harsh emotions, illness, and misery. See if your words ever convey failure, hopelessness, despair, criticism, or judgment. Do you ever say things like, 'I never get what I want,' 'I can't do it,' 'It's no use trying,' or, 'I never have enough money?' Perhaps you worry about things. It doesn't help, but we still do it. Our negative words and actions can influence the people around us, so if we can stop doing this, we help them as well. It will take some determination and self-discipline, but this is true of most valuable goals.

"Michael talked last week about how negative thoughts can cause illness. Our thoughts affect other areas of life as well. I am going to discuss some of these.

"We all think about events in our past. That is normal. But some people live in the past most of the time. They might collect things from a particular period of life, or talk about it a lot. We also think about our future. Perhaps about the holiday or party we've planned for next month. This also is quite normal. But some people spend their life looking forward to the next thing.

"The main reason for thinking a lot about our past or future is because we are not happy in the present. If you do this, see why you are dissatisfied and change it.

"If you are always thinking about the past or what lies ahead, your attention is not in the present. Then you don't see what is happening in front of you. You may miss the various signs you set up to guide you through your life.

"The ideal way is to live now. Then you are in communication with your environment. You are seeing it as it truly is right now. Not as it did exist, even five minutes ago, or as it may exist next week.

"Your thoughts have the power to create what happens to you. All your thoughts, both positive and negative, work like a boomerang. What you send out comes back to you. It's that mirror again. For example, if you think that people are dishonest and try to cheat you, you will probably be cheated. Alternately, if you believe that most people are honest, you will find this is so. If you have kind, loving, positive thoughts, then you will attract people who are kind and loving. Like attracts like. If you criticize people, you will be criticized."

There was a question from the crowd. Devora listened intently. "Thank you. It is an important question," she said. "A gentleman has asked, 'If you can't criticize anyone, how can you ever tell someone he or she is doing something wrong?'

"Constructive opinion, when genuinely needed, can be given in a positive and loving way. Perhaps we can check that the comment we are about to make is both intuitive and loving, and not coming from our mind or ego. A lot of our views about right or wrong can be opinions or beliefs we have picked up from other people. When we see someone behave in a particular way, we often, without thinking, try to enforce on them the rules of what we believe is acceptable behavior. Sometimes we correct people because we want to seem clever or important, or we want to make them feel bad for doing something that we believe to be wrong.

"Yes, it does take courage to always act from our hearts. We have to be honest with ourselves. Is what we are about to say or do truly loving or helpful? Our spiritual nature is a positive one. Once we retrain ourselves to be positive in thought and action, we won't need to check anymore. Does that answer the question?

"The thoughts you have most often determine the type of energy that is around you. Positive thoughts create a light and happy energy, and make you pleasant to be around. If you are positive, you enjoy life more. Because others feel comfortable with you, you have more friends. You usually feel better after talking to someone with a sunny outlook. Negative thoughts create a dense, heavy energy that makes positive people feel uncomfortable in such an environment.

"It is possible to be cheerful, no matter the circumstances. Many people experience tragic circumstances and yet remain positive. They could just as easily have become bitter. There is always a choice. Why not decide to be positive? Your life will certainly change for the better. I can recommend it," she said smiling.

"Speaking of choosing to think positively brings me to the subject of next week's discussion. It is about the choices you have in life.

"We will see you on Sunday. Have a lovely evening."

Choice

Everyone has the power of choice

You have a right to choose

You make choices every moment of your life

You can always change your mind or choose differently

You can make perfect choices using your intuition

The most important choice is to be yourself

You can choose to follow your own will or Divine Will

· Chapter 12 ·

Choice

The people who had been attending the talks for a while were feeling a real bond as they shared this new wisdom. Some of them felt they had found the pot of gold at the end of the rainbow. They were beginning to understand. There was an inner excitement about it all. They all felt much more confident and positive about life these days.

With the understanding that was growing each week came a greater trust of these nine people who had suddenly become a special part of their lives. Slowly, as the weeks went by, the people began to soften to the idea that they were really being helped. It hadn't been an easy couple of months, but it became less and less confusing as time went on. The people knew they were getting closer to being able to explain this wonderful knowledge to their friends and family.

Many of those who had originally complained loudly of the intrusion into their lives were now silent. They had changed their minds as they began to see the difference in the way they all dealt with each other. For example, in the first few weeks there was very little communication taking place and certainly no thought of sharing food. There had been a lot of pushing and arguing about where to sit. It was quite changed now. People chatted to each other with the ease of long-term friends. There was lots of fun and laughter along with the sharing of the food. And everyone took care to make sure they didn't block the view of those behind them.

One of the nine now stood up and moved forward to speak. Everyone had seen this man sitting in the group, but he had not spoken to them before. "My name is Scott." His voice was rich and mellow. They liked him immediately. "As Devora mentioned, this week we are going to talk about the choices each of us make.

"Everyone has the power of choice ,
You have a right to choose,
You make choices every moment of your life,
You can always change your mind or choose differently,
You can make perfect choices using your intuition,
The most important choice is to be yourself,
You can choose to follow your own will or Divine Will.

"You have the power to change your life. We all make choices in every moment of our lives. For example, you are continually choosing whether to love, trust, help, judge, be responsible, or become involved—or not. You choose to live with integrity or deception, to speak or be silent, to create harmony or discord, to be still or active, calm or noisy, to be truthful or lie, to be courageous or fearful, and whether to live in a balanced way or be 'up in the clouds.' You chose whether to come here today.

"You choose whether you are going to be in control of your destiny or a victim of it, to be with a certain person or group, to be in one location or another, and whether to think or act in a positive or negative way. You have a choice whether to communicate or not, whether by touch or words.

"You choose how you view the world. You may see it as a place of great beauty, where nature presents us with a parade of wondrous landscapes—a world where the majority of people live in peace and harmony. Alternately, you may see it as a materialistic world, full of wars, turmoil, illness, and starving people. Both exist. You decide where to focus your attention.

"This doesn't mean you have to pretend there are no negative aspects to life. You could even help to change them, if you want. It may excite you to join a group that serves soup to homeless people. You can do this with cheery optimism, or you can complain that your hard work is not appreciated.

"Positive behavior connects us to the natural flow and order that exists in the world. It is like swimming with the tide and not against it. The struggle and effort that many associate with life disappears when we are 'in the flow.'

"Another important choice we have in each moment is whether or not to follow our intuition. We often organize our lives doing what we think we *should* do. We rush around trying to control everything, too busy to listen to our inner spiritual guidance. We are all intuitive, but we don't always listen to this inner teaching. Sometimes we follow our emotions or thoughts.

"When you don't listen to your intuition, you can break an agreement or promise you made. I will give you an example. Let's say that in the plans you made before you incarnated, you arranged to meet a particular person. This person was going to be born in a different country. So together you planned that you would travel to that country and would meet up. You plan the trip and you are excited about going. But your partner or parent does not want you to go. You feel guilty about leaving them, so you cancel the trip. The agreement you made has now been broken. It may be that you never meet this person. This can affect both your lives.

"You may find you are really disappointed that you didn't go on the trip. Hopefully, this feeling will be sufficient to never again be put off from doing what you truly want.

"Sometimes the same situation happens many times before we finally learn. How often have we said to ourselves, 'When will I learn to say no?' 'Why do I keep compromising?' 'Why do I communicate with them, when I don't want to?' 'Why do I choose the same type of partner again and again?' But each time it happens to us, we are closer to learning. Finally, we are determined not to let it happen again, and the lesson is learned.

"From a spiritual perspective, it doesn't matter how long you take to learn something. You have all the time in the world. It's your choice as to how long you take. It is no one else's concern but yours. Of course, it does make life a lot easier for everyone involved when you learn quickly. It helps when you begin to trust your inner guidance.

"Sometimes it may seem that there is no choice available. An important point to remember is that the choice may have been made in the planning stage, prior to birth. You might think that people who lack education don't have a choice of what job they do. But education, or the lack of it, will have been chosen prior to birth, to give people the learning they need. A limited education may also provide a good challenge. For example, many people with major reading difficulties, and little or no education, have found a way around this and become very successful. People without the opportunity to be educated as children, often manage to educate themselves as adults. Perhaps they grow stronger and more wise in the process!

"Everyone has a right to choose how they wish to live, as well as where and with whom. Ideally we could allow people to do what feels right to them, and not inflict our own ideas of what they should be doing. Try to let people be themselves, without judging and criticizing, or trying to decide what is best for them. Of course, in order to live harmoniously, a certain integrity and way of behaving is necessary.

"We can give advice or encourage certain types of behavior. It often feels right to do this. Children, family, and friends need guidance and support, just as we do. But it is so easy to automatically pass on the conditioning we have received during our lives. Sometimes it seems that our minds are bottomless pits of opinions about everything. We often say and do things because we feel that society expects it of us. But how often do we check if we truly believe what we are saying? Give advice from the heart, and give it in a loving way.

"On a larger scale, we can make a choice about the sort of world we want to live in. It may be surprising, but people do choose the type of world they live in. For example, if we didn't watch violent films or buy newspapers, none would be made. If we chose not to pay taxes or to receive monies from taxes, taxes would not exist. If we no longer wanted to be ruled by governments, we would not vote and there would be no government. If we chose not to pay high prices for a particular service, the price would rapidly fall. The power of choice is always in the hands of the people.

"That is all I 'choose' to say on this subject," he said, smiling. "I hope this has given you an idea of the importance of choice.

"I would like to end this evening with something a little different. You are all capable of great inner peace. When you find that peace, you can hear your inner guidance.

"Some people here may have heard of something called meditation. We are going to do this now. This helps to quiet the mind and align with the intuitive spiritual nature. It won't take long. I promise we will still finish in time for the usual transport home. So, just enjoy it." He paused and had a drink of water.

"Please make yourself comfortable. You may wish to spread out a little to give yourselves more space. Some may prefer to lie down. I will increase the microphone level so you will all be able to hear, no matter how far away you go. When we are finished, you should feel more peaceful and relaxed."

People began moving and re-arranging themselves. Those who were used to meditation had no problem in quickly finding a space to lie down. Encouraged by them, others also began to lie down.

Scott waited until they were all settled. "I know this is new to many of you, but it is not difficult to do. It's just a form of relaxation. Decide you have nothing else to do than be here, enjoying the beauty all around you. Let go of all the thoughts in your head.

"Let go. Allow your head and shoulders to relax. Release any tightness from your neck and back. Let your arms and legs go loose. Now let your whole body relax."

He began slowly and quietly. His voice had a soothing, tranquil quality. "Let your mind drift into stillness. You are walking in a beautiful meadow in the countryside, surrounded by flowers. The warm sun is streaming down on your face. You can see for miles across the hills. There is no one to be seen anywhere. Nothing is stirring. Your mind is quiet and you are enjoying the perfect silence of the moment. There is nowhere else in the world you need to be. You are at peace with the world.

"You decide to lie down in the grass. You look up at the blue sky above. You feel the stillness of the space all around you. In the silence, you are aware only of a soft breeze, carrying the perfume of wild roses, as it whispers through the leaves on the trees. You watch the white puffy clouds slowly moving across the sky. You can feel the grass and the ground beneath your body. Stretch your body out to its fullest extent. Now let it go limp and be completely relaxed. All the different parts of your body are in balance and harmony with each other.

"Close your eyes. Feel yourself floating as though you were one of those clouds. You are completely safe.

You are drifting gently, becoming a part of a huge ocean of peace. Remain peaceful and let my words reach deep inside you.

"I am at peace with myself. I am at peace with all my brothers and sisters in this huge family of humankind. My mind is quiet. My thoughts are at peace, my inner world is calm. My existence is peace. I am the essence of peace and love.

"I move through time and space with ease. From this wonderful place of peace, I begin my journey. I fly silently upward and outward, far beyond the material world of time and motion. I fly beyond Earth into the dimensions of Light. My home is uninterrupted silence—a vast ocean of stillness. I am at peace within this silence. I am a child at the shore's edge and I enter into the ocean smoothly and easily, like a bird gliding on a current. I move to the center of the ocean. I see a great Light radiating throughout the world. I touch the point of Light and I become still. The vibrations of Light move through me and I am radiating Light.

"I am full of love, care, and compassion for all my family—the whole world. I release the past and move to the now. I am free. I am still, steady, and balanced in peace. I see from this place of peace that all things are passing. I can change anything. I see the natural flow of destiny. I align myself with the natural Divine order of the world. I see my perfect place in that natural order. I become the peace of the world. I am still and in harmony with all things. I see the perfection of the world. I am content. I understand my life and I trust in the wisdom of my higher self. I am guided perfectly in all that I do. I relax and enjoy my life in every moment. I am joyful and loving. All is well in my world. I feel the calm and the silence within. I take this calm and peace into the world wherever I go."

He paused, allowing some minutes of silence. Softly, he continued. "That is the end of the meditation. I want you to gently become aware of being here in the park. Remaining calm and peaceful, slowly begin to bring your attention back to the park. If you are sitting, gently feel the ground beneath your feet. If you are lying down, feel your body against the ground. Keep doing this until you feel you are here with us in the park. When you are ready, open your eyes. Take your time, there is no hurry. Take a few minutes to get your bearings. If you are lying down, you may like to sit up. It can help to have a drink or to eat something.

"When you stand up, your balance may be different for a few moments. If you feel a little unsteady, it means you are not sufficiently in the present moment yet. Just keep feeling your feet on the ground and perhaps have something else to eat or drink.

"I see that you are all back with us now. What you have just felt can be achieved any time you seek peace and tranquillity in your life. You can do the same thing at home by playing soft music and allowing yourself to become still. It is by getting in touch with the peace and stillness within that you can find yourself.

"That is all for this evening. As you see, we have finished at the normal time." People began looking at their watches and were surprised to see that indeed they had. It felt like much longer. He smiled. "Next week, we will speak about truth."

Truth

The communication of truth solves everything

Until exact truth is viewed, situations remain unresolved

Truth is the exact who, what, when, and why of something

Truth is relative to the awareness of the individual

As you grow in wisdom, higher levels of truth are seen

All truth can be found through the connection to Spirit

Say what you mean and mean what you say

· CHAPTER 13 ·

Truth

The park was packed once again. The crowd finally settled. It was a different member of the nine who stood up this week. He was much taller than the others, with light brown hair falling across his forehead and the most amazing blue eyes. He was laughing as he tossed the hair from his face, giving the impression of a young boy with not a care in the world. The joy showing in his face was infectious. It lit their hearts and made them smile.

"Hello. My name is Dennis. I see from the increasing number of hampers each week that you are determined not to starve. It is so wonderful to see you enjoying yourselves. Sometimes we pass by here some hours after we have finished our talk. We see many of you continuing to enjoy the warm evenings and pleasant company. It is a lovely place to have a picnic by the lake. Perhaps we have started a trend that will continue long after we are gone," he said smiling.

"Today I would like to talk to you about truth.

"The communication of truth solves everything,
Until exact truth is viewed, situations remain unresolved,

Truth is the exact who, what, when, and why of something,
Truth is relative to the awareness of the individual,
As you grow in wisdom, higher levels of truth are seen,
All truth can be found through the connection to Spirit,
Say what you mean and mean what you say.

"Although truth is so valuable to us, it has become acceptable in our society to tell lies. We do this to cover up what we see as our mistakes, to hide our true feelings, or to gain what we think is an advantage. But it can end up working against us. How often do we see that a truthful approach early on might have prevented us years of anguish?

"There are many factors involved with truth, so we will begin with a definition. We could say that the truth of something would be exactly what happened, who was involved, and when and where it occurred.

"Why do we need to know the truth? You are here on Earth to learn. When you get a false picture of something, you can't learn. So to be able to learn from any problem or situation, you have to know the why and how of it. And you will hold onto the situation until you do. It stays with you, often through many lifetimes, buried in your subconscious. You might think it is resolved, and you may never think about it, but one day it comes back. You will hold on to the thoughts, emotions, decisions, and outcome connected with it, until you find out the truth.

"A lot of what we think of as truth are just beliefs we have adopted from friends, family, education, and the media. When things happen to us, we judge them through the beliefs we hold. If, for example, we believed the statistics that said two out of three marriages will end in divorce, we add that negative possibility to our own marriage prospects. If we had never heard of such a thing occurring, would we even consider the possibility?

"Our life situation, and the experiences we have, color what we see. Imagine for example, that a charity fete is planned. There are going to be pony rides, children's races and other games. Everyone is hoping for a lovely sunny day to encourage lots of people to come to the fete. Shortly before it is due to open, the sky darkens and it pours with rain for the rest of the day. Everything is washed out and very few people come. The organizers and participants all express their extreme disappointment. When asked, they will probably say that Saturday was a terrible day. Their personal memory of July that year may even be colored by this one day of bad weather. This was their experience. This was true for them.

"However, a few miles away, as the dark clouds were appearing in the sky, the local farmers began to hope and pray. As the rain poured down, a lot of very happy farmers began celebrating. At last, enough rain was falling to make a difference to their crops and water reserves. This was their experience concerning the rain that day. For them, that summer was wonderful. This is how we can arrive at different truths depending on our experiences.

"However, truth also changes depending on the awareness of the individual. Let's say your partner vanishes and you are left with no means of support to care for your young family. You would probably feel that this is a bad thing that has happened to you. This is true. But, it is a truth based on a particular level of awareness.

"What if you understood the higher reason for this happening? I wonder if you would still think it was bad? What if you now remembered that when you were reviewing your last lifetime, you saw that you often 'gave up' when challenged by life's obstacles. You decided you wanted to fix this. You needed to become stronger. So, as you planned this current life, you included a situation to help you gain this. You thought that having a young family to fight for might help you overcome your weakness of giving up. So now this situation has arrived, and it seems 'bad' to you. Incidentally, the children involved would have also agreed to this situation, for their own learning. You will recall that all family members make plans together about what is to occur—before they enter the lifetime.

"So, if you knew this higher picture, would you still think that what happened was bad? Or would you understand that a good thing had happened to you? In fact, one that was quite essential to help you achieve the strength you desire.

"Do you see how truth differs depending on where you are looking from? As we explained before, each of us deliberately forgets the plans we made before we were born. We do this because the way we learn is through having things unexpectedly happen in our lives. We gain in strength and wisdom by overcoming the obstacles. We don't need to know the higher reason for something occurring. As we said, it benefits us not to know. But keeping in mind the fact that there is always a higher picture can help us learn more quickly.

"Everything that happens in the world has a higher picture or reason. When you begin to trust in that, it helps to keep things in a better perspective. It helps us stay more calm and balanced and not to get so caught up in the anguish of the moment. You can say to yourself, 'I may not understand why this is happening, but I will trust in the higher order of things.'

"That's all for this week. I hope what I have said will give you a different viewpoint to work with. Truth can be a great healer.

"Next week we will speak about love and your relationships—and about the different types of love there are."

Love

Pure love is accepting others just as they are

It is possible to love everyone

Unconditional love is the highest form of love

The ability to love is our greatest gift

Love carries Light to the world

A relationship is right, if we can learn and grow from it

If it no longer feels right, it may be time to move on

· Chapter 14 ·

Love

The number of people now gathering for the weekly talk had greatly increased. This meant a lot of people were now seated on areas of lawn far from the platform. A microphone had been set up some weeks ago in anticipation of this. It was powerful enough so the people sitting farthest away could hear clearly.

Devora rose from the chair and stood quietly, waiting for them to settle.

They felt the same love coming from her that had relaxed them all three weeks ago. That was the evening they thought it would rain. Instead, it had been quite beautiful, with a clear, star-studded sky. The disappearance of the dark clouds that day seemed to be connected with the love they felt from her. It somehow got across the message about the power of positive thinking she had spoken of that evening.

"I am happy to be giving a talk today about love. It's such a wonderful subject! I think we all agree that love really does make the world go 'round. It seems to be something we all want and strive for, although for many, it does seem elusive at times. We wish to tell you our ideas about love. It may help you see you are much more loved than you realize.

"Pure love is accepting others just as they are,
It is possible to love everyone,
Unconditional love is the highest form of love,
The ability to love is our greatest gift,
Love carries Light to the world,
A relationship is right, if we can learn and grow from it,
If it no longer feels right, it may be time to move on.

"Of all our experiences in life, I'm sure you will agree that relationships are probably the most difficult, and perhaps the most rewarding! There are so many different aspects—they probably give us our greatest learning.

"We can learn through the sharing and exchange involved in all types of relationships, whether they be romantic, sexual, or those of friendship or support. Much can be gained through experiencing the harmony, freedom, tolerance and patience that are part of all relationships. We can learn about giving and receiving, and how to find a balance between the two.

"Love can be based on a physical, emotional, mental or spiritual level. All relationships involve one or more of these four areas. You can be physically attracted to someone. Perhaps you are emotionally bonded in some way. You could find someone's intellect or intelligence stimulating. Most of our difficulties and learning occur in the first three of the four areas.

"Then there is the spiritually based relationship—the least difficult one. This form of love involves a wonderful interplay of unconditional love at its highest level. It is a relationship of nonjudgment, where everything is understood and forgiven. There is no expecting, demanding, needing, or wanting to change anything. It is a selfless love; a giving, allowing, and willingness to spend time getting it right. Everything is harmonious.

"We often see this sort of love between a parent and child. We see the many allowances a parent gives a child, forgiving their behavior and mistakes. This bond of *unconditional love* often remains between a parent and child throughout their lives. However sometimes, as the child grows up, the allowances previously given are withdrawn. Some of us decide that because they are no longer children, they shouldn't make mistakes anymore. Now they fall into the category where we often place other people—one of *conditional* love. This is the type of love where we decide we will only love people 'if they behave as we think they should.' If they behave otherwise, they become unlovable. We criticize and judge them for their behavior. This may be for the moment or the long term.

"We see acts of unconditional love all over the world. There are many beautiful and genuine gifts of selfless service given by others and ourselves every day. There are also times when what seems to be selfless service can be someone being a martyr or victim, or someone trying to look good. We often see unconditional love in the relationship we have with animals, such as with a dog. Even beaten and starved, a dog will usually remain loyal and loving to its owner.

"Unconditional love is an ability we attain. It comes when a higher understanding is reached. As we grow in our wisdom, we realize the differences we see in the many nationalities, races, religions, customs, and beliefs on Earth, are all helping to make up the wonderful richness of our lives. They are not a reason for separation. We come to realize the criticisms and judgments we make about others come only from our ignorance.

"Our society, and even we, place restrictions on who we can or will love. We create a multitude of barriers, particularly in our romantic relationships. We have accepted beliefs that we should date or marry within our own background, education, social and financial position, nationality, local community, race, religion, and age group. We also adopt restrictions concerning the right 'looks,' weight, accent, height, physique, and sometimes even eye and hair color! Quite restrictive, isn't it? With all the conditions we put in the way, it's surprising we establish any partnerships at all.

"A relationship of any kind is only beneficial for as long as it feels right. When it no longer serves us, when the lessons are ended and, despite our searching, we can find no meaning in it, then it is surely time to move on. This means there may come a point in any relationship, whether it is a friendship, romance, or business partnership, when the exchange you both wished to give each other is completed.

"The institution of marriage is another word for relationship. Some are destined to last a lifetime. Others for just a short while. Our intuitive knowing will tell us when a relationship is meant to end. In regard to divorce, we could say that if there is no longer a real marriage of heart and soul, perhaps it is time for both parties to move on.

"Friends give us advice about what we should and shouldn't do. However, it is difficult for other people to see what is or isn't being gained by any relationship. They may see a marriage that appears to be one-sided and conclude that one partner is not benefiting. What is actually happening may not be obvious. We choose many things that do not seem to make sense consciously. It could be that some people have chosen partners who will 'walk all over them,' in order to learn inner strength or self-esteem. It may take years to learn a particular lesson. Sometimes it takes a lot of being pushed, before we realize we deserve better—before we stand up for ourselves and say, 'enough!' Perhaps the person who appears to be receiving nothing has chosen to support the other person in this life. Perhaps the positions were reversed in their last lifetime together. It doesn't matter how long it takes to learn. There is no time limit set for these things.

"We have all heard that giving is better than receiving. And it seems to work this way. Giving help is a wonderful form of love. When it comes from the heart and feels right to help, it is a beautiful act of compassion. It also makes us feel better. And because life is a mirror, if we give help, we then attract people into our lives who will help us.

"However, sometimes we help because we feel we must. Perhaps you thought you were the only person available at the time. Maybe you didn't want to look bad in the eyes of your friends. This type of help does not come from the heart.

"If you are giving help because you should, it won't excite you or feel right. Your lack of interest and excitement is showing you, in that instance, that giving help is not in Divine Order. When helping doesn't feel right, but you do it anyway, you are not actually helping. This is because, from a spiritual perspective and higher picture, you were not meant to help then. You are actually able to feel when your help will benefit someone and when it won't.

"We might not have a logical reason for not wanting to help. All we know is that we don't want to. It doesn't excite us. We can learn to trust our inner responses. As a society, we often feel guilty about things, such as not helping. Then we try to find acceptable reasons to explain our behavior to our friends.

"I would help only when it feels right to do so. For example, I would not automatically assist an elderly person across a busy road. Sometimes it may feel right, and other times not. I don't ask myself for a logical reason as to why I don't want to help. I have learned to trust my feelings. I know there will be a higher reason for me not helping. I don't need to know what that is. Perhaps it will help the person grow stronger. This may be an opportunity for that person to realize he or she is not weak or incapable of doing this alone. It could be that someone else is meant to help this person. If you try this for yourself, you will soon see that sometimes nonaction can be just as helpful as action. When you help because you feel obliged to do so, the people sense this. This help can make them feel worse. It can make people believe they are weak or a burden to us.

"Helping or not helping, provided it comes from the heart and we expect nothing in return, is unconditional love. When we trust our heart to lead us, we will act correctly.

"There is another way to look at the meaning of love. Remember the planning that people do before they are born? And how people arrange different circumstances to help in their learning? Well, let's say that in your plan for this life you included a partner who is going to leave you, in order to teach you greater inner strength. Or maybe after seeing that you often abandoned people who needed you in your last life, you chose to be abandoned yourself to see what it feels like to be on the receiving end. So, would it not be an act of love when your partner leaves you? Might your assumption that your partner no longer loves you be incorrect?

"Looking at it from this perspective, perhaps a lot of what we see in the world is actually done through love. You may like to think a little more about that later. Once you begin to understand love from this higher perspective, you may see that people are helping each other all over the planet.

"Love wins through anything. It can transcend pain and sorrow, confusion, loneliness, hopelessness, and despair. It brings health, energy, and youth. This most magnificent and exquisite gift is the power that holds families, worlds, and universes together. It is the single greatest source of forgiveness. Love solves everything. Pure love is the mightiest force in the Universe.

"The Light of the world is carried through love. Within the wisdom of love, we see that each of us holds a unique silken thread to the Tapestry of Life. Each single thread is necessary to make it all perfect.

"Perhaps love is the truth we have lost along the way.

"Next week we will discuss a special energy we have around our bodies and how it assists us in our lives."

The Aura

An aura is an energy field of color around a body

Every living thing has an aura

The aura colors show our current state of being

A strong colorful aura assists good health

The aura acts as a protective cloak for the body

Auras are strengthened by positive thought

Auras are weakened by negative thoughts

· CHAPTER 15 ·

The Aura

This time it was Mark who addressed the crowd. "I'm going to talk about something you can't see, and have probably never heard of, but you all have one." He smiled as the crowd began laughing. "I am speaking of energy called the aura. Although we can't see it, it is just as important as the other unseen energies we have around us, such as electricity and radio waves.

"An aura is an energy field of color around a body,
Every living thing has an aura,
The aura colors show our current state of being,
A strong colorful aura assists good health,
The aura acts as a protective cloak for the body,
Auras are strengthened by positive thought,
Auras are weakened by negative thoughts.

"Your physical body has energy around it that you cannot see. It is similar in shape to your physical body. It is called an aura. Everything living has an aura, including plants and animals. Some people can see auras, but for most of us, they remain unseen, just the same as television, microwave and satellite frequencies do.

"The aura is a mirror image of what is going on inside the body. This is the same idea as when we see symptoms on our bodies that show us that we have an illness or physical condition inside the body. The aura changes in size. It can become larger or smaller, depending on how expansive or contracted we feel. It also acts as a protective coat against external pollution and negativity.

"The aura is made up of all the colors in the rainbow. These colors vary in shade and intensity, depending on the individual's state of being. Different colors show how you are doing—emotionally, mentally, and physically. For example, if your throat were completely healthy in all three aspects, the aura color around your neck would be a rich blue. However, if you had a sore throat, or found it difficult to talk to people, or if you got 'choked up' emotionally, this color would change to duller shades of blue, or even pale gray. If there were a more severe condition present, such as throat cancer, the color would be dark gray or black.

"Negative thoughts have a vast effect on the state of your aura. In fact, thoughts affect your entire life. When we realize how harmful our negative thoughts can be to ourselves and the planet, it can make us more determined to live a positive life. Negative thoughts produce bitterness, illness, and misery. They make the aura weak, as do drugs, alcohol, and physical damage to the body.

"A weak aura leaves us open to negative energies. These may come from people, places, pollution, or chemicals in our environment. So it's important not to be critical. Be aware of your thoughts. 'I can't do it,' is negative. If you think like this, you could decide to change.

"It is possible to repair a weakened aura. There are several methods you can use. Nature provides healing for every condition that can occur in life. Many of the natural remedies found in plants and flowers will strengthen your aura. These are called flower essences and can be purchased quite easily. There are many books written about this. We will be talking more about nature's healing later.

"You can think positively. You can use positive affirmations. These are statements that help us think the right way, such as, 'I am in good health.' Another technique that helps maintain a strong aura is to imagine white light flooding down through your body.

"It is ideal to keep your aura in top condition. The best way to do this is by living in a positive, loving, and harmonious way. This keeps you healthy and makes you a well-balanced, capable, loving person who enjoys life. Your aura radiates with beautiful clear colors, which in turn creates a healthy mind and body.

"Other people can sense the radiations that come from our aura. The energy they are sensing is often referred to as *vibrations*. If your aura is colorful and strong, people will experience a sense of well-being in your presence. People won't feel comfortable near someone whose aura is weak and colorless.

"I hope this information is sufficient to give you an idea of how you can help yourself stay healthy. Next week we will discuss the subject of color and how it can help you in your life."

Colors affect us physically, mentally, and spiritually

Color is a wonderful healer

The right colors enhance health and well-being

Different colors heal different things

Each color has its own frequency, similar to a TV signal

We benefit from wearing clothes in colors we like

It is possible to have too much or too little of a color

· CHAPTER 16 ·

Color

It was a new member of the group who stood up and moved toward the microphone. Soft chestnut hair framed her gentle face. Her beautiful dress was a blending of all the pastel shades of the rainbow. She had a slight build and appeared quite delicate. Yet, when she spoke there was great strength in her voice.

"Hello, my name is Carris. This week we want to talk about some aspects of color that may be unfamiliar to many of you. Color can help us in many areas of our lives.

"Colors affect us physically, mentally and spiritually,
Color is a wonderful healer,
The right colors enhance health and well-being,
Different colors heal different things,
Each color has its own frequency, similar to a TV signal,
We benefit from wearing clothes in colors we like,
It is possible to have too much or too little of a color.

"Color is one of the greatest healing tools available on Earth. It can help us recover from emotional traumas, mental breakdowns, and physical illness. Those colors we feel drawn to will give us strength and balance on a physical, mental, and emotional level. Each color contains a different quality of energy that can help us in different areas of our well-being.

"Although you may not realize it, you often intuitively know which colors will help you. You may instinctively reach for the right colors to wear, but ignore this feeling and select something practical. In the future, when you get dressed, instead of thinking about what you should wear, see if you are drawn to a particular color or combination of colors. You will feel much better in colors that are right for you. You don't normally look good or feel comfortable in colors you don't like.

"It is beneficial to choose the right colors for everything you have around you. As well as your clothes, the colors that you use in your home and workplace can help to create a feeling of well-being. The furnishings and decorations you use make a difference. Choosing colors you like will create a harmonious and peaceful place to live. You might think that the color of one piece of furniture is not going to matter very much. But sometimes it can make a difference to the overall feeling of a room. If you have a favorite room where you like to relax, have a look at why you feel comfortable there. Have you noticed there is often one room in a house where visitors and family gather? It might not even be the most physically comfortable. Although there may be comfortable armchairs in the next room, guests often happily chat while sitting on hard kitchen work surfaces! They are responding to the energy of the room. The energy is created through the use of color.

"Some places make us feel uncomfortable. We don't like to linger for long in a room that is painted in clashing or inharmonious colors. It could be just one item in the room that doesn't harmonize. If you find your guests are rushing off before the dessert, you could check the colors in your home," Carris said laughing.

"You can also benefit from choosing your car in a color you like. We can spend a lot of time in our car. Even if we don't use it, it is often within sight. So, next time you get a car, as well as looking at its performance, you could also think about its color!" she said smiling.

"Your needs tend to change, so different colors may be needed at different times. The need alters depending on your current emotional, mental and physical state. It is also important to use the right amount of a color around you. It is possible to have too much of a particular color. For example, you may find you are drawn to red when your energy is low. So wearing red clothing would see your energy restored. However, if you went on wearing red after your energy had returned, you could start to become angry, hyperactive, or aggressive. If you find you can comfortably wear red a lot of the time, it may mean you are in constant need of energy. Perhaps you could check if something is draining your energy. This can happen if you are in a job or situation you don't enjoy. Alternately, too little of a color you need won't be enough to correct the condition.

"A person who felt a need to decorate a room mostly in blue would eventually gain the sense of peace and balance needed. However, once peace was restored, the person could end up being depressed from the continued presence of blue, and even begin to dislike the color. They would probably not realize it was the source of the depression! If you feel a desire to wear blue all the time, or are quite comfortable living in a room painted blue, it may mean you live in an inharmonious environment and have a constant need for peace.

"If you feel drawn toward green, it could mean, on an emotional level, that you are in need of a healing of the heart. Or it could mean you are physically unwell. On a mental level, it can be an indication of feeling 'crowded in'—either at work, home, or with life in general. Green gives a feeling of space. This is why walking in nature provides a wonderful feeling of well-being. You would also need green if you were a dreamy and inattentive person. It gives a grounding effect and helps bring you back to Earth. You may feel comfortable with lots of green around, because you have an ability to heal people or animals.

"A desire for a lot of white can show a need for purity or cleansing on some level. It can also show a comfort and ease with spiritual areas. Orange helps us with new ideas and physical activity. It is excellent for recovering from shock. Placing some orange material around someone who has had a shock will absorb the shock from the person's aura and will help to heal the shock.

"Yellow helps our clarity of mind. So, yellow is ideal for anyone who is studying. Gold helps with wisdom, confidence, and the qualities we associate with a masculine energy. Silver helps with the feminine energies of intuition, caring, and compassion. Wearing black may show we feel a need to disappear into the crowd.

"There is a lot more to this subject. Each color has many more healing qualities than I have mentioned today. However, you will find there are many books and organizations dealing with color as a healing tool. I wish you all a brilliantly colorful life," she said smiling warmly.

"Thank you, and good night. We will see you next week."

The Common Cold

The common cold is caused by a loss

A cold replaces your loss

It is the "thought" of losing something
that causes the cold

The loss can be a person, place, object,
or situation

Each of us has a different idea of what
a loss is

It may be a real loss or an imagined one

Finding the thought that caused it,
ends the cold

· CHAPTER 17 ·

The Common Cold

"Hello, my name is Scott."

The people who were still sorting out their food hampers, looked up surprised. They hadn't realized that he was starting to talk. They were reminded again how lovely his rich, mellow voice was. They settled their things quickly, not wanting to miss a word.

"My last talk was about the choices each of us has in life. This week I am going to talk about something else you have probably had at one time or another. They can be quite a nuisance. I am talking about colds—ordinary, everyday colds.

"A lot of time and money has been spent trying to find a cure for the common cold. Special testing establishments for this purpose have operated for many years. People are paid to stay at these places as volunteers. During their stay, they are deliberately exposed to conditions that encourage them to catch a cold. The studies have been interesting, but unsuccessful. This is because the real cause of colds is not known.

"We felt that most of you have personal experience of colds. So we thought we would use this to give you a little more understanding of how science and spirituality go hand in hand.

"The common cold is caused by a loss,
A cold replaces your loss,
It is the "thought" of losing something that causes the cold,
The loss can be a person, place, object, or situation,
Each of us has a different idea of what a loss is,
It may be a real loss or an imagined one,
Finding the thought that caused it, ends the cold.

"A cold is caused by a loss. This doesn't apply to a cold that is accompanied by a cough or sore throat. This has been covered in our talk on illness.

"The loss may be a physical one, such as losing a purse or wallet. It may be a mental loss, such as feeling your freedom is being restricted. It could be a 'loss of face' that we have when we are embarrassed. The loss may or may not actually happen. It is your thought that it has happened or will happen that is the important factor here. So it is not the actual loss, but the *thought* of it that causes the cold.

"We only experience a sense of loss when we believe that something we really need has gone from our life. A loss can mean different things to different people. Some people feel a sense of loss if a friend is cross with them or if they miss their favorite TV program. Someone else may not feel a loss unless their house burns down or their family dies. Some people never feel a sense of loss. In this case, they would never get a cold.

"Cold and damp conditions seem to cause a cold. However, the cause is not getting wet. It's the loss we get from feeling we are no longer warm and comfortable. People often get a cold after returning from a holiday. If they have been in a warmer climate, they blame the colder weather. But instead of cold weather being the cause, they are missing the holiday sun. They might also be missing the freedom they had from their daily work and responsibilities. Perhaps they miss the excitement and lack of inhibitions they felt while being away from home.

"To cure the cold, you have to find the thought that started it. If you find the exact thought you had that gave you a feeling of loss, the cold will disappear instantly. It may sound hard to believe, but even a blocked nose can immediately clear. The only way to discover if this works is to try what we suggest.

"When you notice you are getting a cold, ask yourself if you've had some sort of loss in the last week or so. The right answer is usually the one that pops up first. It is easy to miss the first thought you have, so watch for it. Don't complicate things by making long lists of possible losses you may have had. We have a tendency to do this, ignoring the simple answers in life because they seem too easy. We have the idea that for it to be a proper solution, it needs to be difficult and complicated. Yet real truth is always simple.

"So, to handle the cold, it is necessary to find the exact thought you had and not just the general area of the loss. I will give you an example. A grandmother is visited by her daughter and grandchildren. These visits are rare. After they return home, the grandmother gets a cold. You may think, 'Well that's obvious, it must be the family leaving.' It could be. But that could be the general area of the loss. The exact thought is needed in order to make the cold disappear immediately. If only the general area is found, the cold does go, but it follows a different pattern. Initially it seems to get worse, but then clears much faster than it would have otherwise.

"So, the general area could be the family leaving. But, the exact thought may have been something like, 'It was so nice having the children around. They made me feel quite young again.' So, the loss in this case has to do with not feeling young anymore. Or it could be that having her daughter around caused the grandmother to think about her own role as a parent. Maybe she thought, 'I should have given my daughter more attention when she was a child.' In this example, the thought, with its sense of sadness or guilt, would be the loss.

"On a spiritual level, the loss causes a space or emptiness around you. You then try to fill up the space with something. Perhaps a 'cold,' or by treating yourself to a nice meal, or buying something new, like a house!" He laughed as they looked at him in surprise. "I was just checking to see if you were listening," he said. "As I see you are, there are no excuses for getting any more colds! Just notice when you are feeling a bit down and have a quick look at what caused it.

"We often go on a spending spree in order to fill up the space. But there is another, cheaper way. This may sound strange. But you can also fix it by hugging a cushion or pillow. Yes, you may laugh," he said smiling. The merriment got even louder. "You hug it until you feel better. You will be relieved to know this doesn't usually take very long. It may be just minutes, or perhaps a little longer. You can, of course, hug a person instead. But in case it does take a while, choose someone you really like!

"Next week, Diana will discuss how to handle problems occurring in your life. The answer will not be to hug a cushion," he said laughing.

Scott, still smiling, could hear the cushion jokes beginning as he left the stage.

Problems

We are the true source of our problems

Problems are challenges to help us grow

Following our intuition can prevent problems

Staying calm helps us see solutions

Communication solves problems

Intuition gives the best solution to any problem

Not helping can be help

· CHAPTER 18 ·

Problems

It was another beautiful afternoon. The flowers were now in full bloom all around the park and perfume filled the air. The people felt they had been very lucky with the weather. Almost every Sunday had been perfect. Even the day that looked like it might rain had changed into a perfect evening. The people were really enjoying themselves. They had gotten to know each other because of the conversations they had after the talks were over. Being able to discuss things really helped. If there was a point someone didn't understand, others soon helped clarify it. Many were hoping they would continue to meet after all the talks were finished.

The people noticed that the group on stage seemed to be looking for someone. Then they realized that Diana was missing. Scott had said that she would give the talk this week. Well, that was unusual! The people started looking around for her. Then they saw a figure running, or was it dancing?, across the lawns, fair hair flying in the wind. Next minute she was up on the stage, breathless and laughing. In her arms, she held a most beautiful cream-colored, fluffy cat. "Sorry I'm late, but this lovely creature wanted to come to our talk," she said smiling. The people laughed, delighted with her sense of fun. They would have forgiven her anything. There was nothing about her that wasn't completely lovable.

She placed the cat carefully on the ground. It looked up at her and then walked over to Devora and proceeded to settle at her feet. Diana smiled at both of them, seeming to share some sort of understanding with them.

Tossing the windswept hair from her face, Diana now addressed the crowd. "It is some time since I last spoke to you about the experience we have between death and our rebirth. The idea must have seemed strange then. Perhaps you understand it more now? I see lots of nods. Well, that's a relief," she said laughing. "It can take a little while to grasp the overall picture, but eventually it all starts to make sense. Today I am going to talk about problems.

"We are the true source of our problems,
Problems are challenges to help us grow,
Following our intuition can prevent problems,
Staying calm helps us see solutions,
Communication solves problems,
Intuition gives the best solution to any problem,
Not helping can be help.

"I don't think any of us get through life without encountering problems in our relationships. It may be with people at work, family, neighbors, officials, or in our business dealings. We would need to be saints to never have problems with our partners, children, parents, or in-laws. Perhaps I will leave the in-laws alone," she said. The people laughed.

"Every circumstance in life is different, so there is no one answer to handle everything. However, there are some useful overall guidelines that may help. Let's look at a typical problem. Perhaps I will be brave and talk about mothers-in-law. Please understand it is nothing personal," she said smiling.

"Let's look at an example. You go to your mother-in-law's house every Sunday for dinner. You may have been doing this for a while. You don't want to go, but you are afraid that if you don't, it will cause an upset. So you go, even though you would rather be somewhere else. Perhaps anywhere else!" She smiled.

"You have a choice. You can either go or follow your inner voice and say no. Although it doesn't excite you, you choose to go. You decided not to follow your intuition. The main reasons we do this are:

a) We aren't sure our intuition is correct;
b) We don't realize the value of following it;
c) We are so used to doing what our mind says, we don't listen to our hearts anymore;
d) We think it might cause an upset and can't face an emotional scene.

"The most rewarding way to live is to follow your heart or intuition. This is how you can best achieve the goals you planned for your life.

"Following your heart means you move with the natural order that takes place in the world. We can see this most clearly in nature. Our intuition is a part of that natural flow. It shows us what is best for us in that moment to achieve our spiritual growth. Living by our hearts, or by intuition, helps us a great deal. It also helps everyone else concerned. Let me explain.

"I will go back to our mother-in-law example. You might think, 'Well, it may not excite me to go to dinner, but my mother-in-law must feel right about inviting me.' Are you sure? Perhaps her request was not intuitive, but came from her mind or ego. She might be lonely or want to talk to someone. Maybe she is making sure you get at least one decent meal a week! Maybe it has become a habit, or she thinks that this is what families do. She could think there is nothing else to do on Sundays! She might be trying to keep herself busy, so she doesn't have time to examine her own life. Maybe she does it to help her run your life!" Diana began laughing. "Oh dear, I am not going to be very popular with mothers-in-law, am I?

"When something doesn't feel right, this is your sign. This is the time to trust. Be strong and say no. If you say no to the dinner invitation, then you can discover where you are really meant to be on Sundays. So can your mother-in-law. Maybe she is supposed to spend Sundays with someone else. Perhaps she needs this time to reflect on her life. It could be that she needs to find out that she can get through the day without feeling lonely. Perhaps she needs to learn to let go of her emotional reactions to this situation. It could be one or more different things. Fortunately, it is not necessary for you to know what is supposed to happen. You only need to trust that if it feels right, it is right, no matter the reaction of others.

"Making a decision to follow your intuition does not mean you aren't being compassionate. You are not deliberately trying to upset someone. You are trying to do what will best serve everyone involved. Nor are you being selfish. Quite the opposite in fact. Following Divine Order is doing what is in the best interests of all concerned.

"This doesn't mean we should avoid all the unpleasant circumstances in life. Some things that are right for us don't always feel joyful. Ideally, they should, but our minds and egos get in the way and we become confused. For example, we may have a friend who is ill in the hospital. Our egos and minds could be saying, 'I am afraid; I don't like hospitals; the smell makes me sick; I don't want to go.' However, when we push those thoughts aside and tune in to our inner voice, we may see it does 'feel right' for us to go.

"When making these kinds of decisions, thoughts come up, such as, 'I am being selfish,' 'What will they think of me?' or 'I'm not being very compassionate, my partner will be upset with me.' They are thoughts, not valid reasons.

"It helps to say to yourself, 'I will put my fears aside and follow my heart.' This puts you more in control of your thoughts. In fact, if you kept this up for a while, your unpleasant responses would lessen. Then you would be controlling your life, instead of it being controlled by your emotions, mind, or ego.

"Be honest about this. We tend to lose abilities that we abuse. Falsely using an excuse that it doesn't feel right to do something will catch up with you later.

"It's not nice when others are displeased. But if it upsets you, life's mirror must be showing you something. I can hear your thoughts," Diana said laughing. "We know about the mirror, tell us something new. But do you really know it? If you do, you will be looking for the lessons to be learned. If we are reacting to others being angry, it means there is something for us to learn. It could even be to learn to stay calm. Calmness helps us think more clearly than when we are angry or upset.

"That doesn't mean you shouldn't feel any emotion, but constant emotional dramas can be quite draining. The answer is to find a balance in all things in life. It is also best not to suppress or bury your emotions. They never really disappear. They just hide—and come up again later," she said smiling.

"When we have a problem with someone, it seems to make us feel better if we find fault with them. So we may say that they are stupid, immature, or bad. But making judgments doesn't help. It may help if we remember that people have different backgrounds, different experiences, and different information, gathered in this life and earlier ones, that contribute to the way they act or react. People try to do their best, based on their own knowledge and experiences. Let's try to be more tolerant and loving. Remember, if we are tolerant, then others will be tolerant with us. Let's try and put ourselves 'in their shoes' and see how they feel.

"It's easy to become overwhelmed if you have lots of problems at the same time. If you have too many changes, jobs, or problems, write out a list of them, choose one and finish it. If that one seems too big, just handle one part of it.

"You may find it hard to resolve a problem when someone has said something about you and you aren't aware of it. If a situation isn't resolving, you could check this. Perhaps someone has believed an untruth about you.

"Sometimes all that is needed to solve a problem is a little more communication. Talking something over gives you more information to help resolve it.

"No matter how big the problem, you can always run away from it," she paused. Some people looked surprised and others began laughing. "I just wanted to see if you were listening," she said smiling. "Okay, no matter how big the problem, it can be handled. No matter how terrible it seems, you will get through it. You never need to do anything as drastic as to take your own life. The pain and anguish make it hard to see the situation clearly, so try to put some attention on something else. Helping someone is always a good remedy.

"Many people see themselves as innocent victims of life's circumstances. But blaming others won't solve anything. You may think you are not responsible, but what about the higher picture? Instead of seeing yourself as a victim, accept responsibility for what happens to you. It won't resolve unless you do. You can try to bury it, and you might even think it is handled, but all the thoughts and feelings will stay with you until you accept your part in it. Some people stay bitter for years, because they continue to blame others for events that have happened to them.

"Situations start to resolve from the moment you say, 'I did this.' This is because you cause the things that happen in your life. A sweeping statement perhaps, but a true one. You may think, 'There is no way I would have wished this to happen.' But remember, there is a higher purpose to your life. Perhaps it has offered you a chance to grow in some way.

"Accepting responsibility for things in our lives doesn't mean we should feel bad or guilty. That doesn't help at all. What does help is a calm acceptance of the part we each play in the creation of our lives. I know the idea that we are responsible for what happens in life is difficult to grasp. It is such an unpopular theory; it takes courage to accept the idea. It is so much easier to blame others. But that won't bring us the happiness we want. When we understand that life is a learning process, then we look at situations differently. We can see that we have wonderful opportunities to grow. Otherwise, we see ourselves as having no control over our lives. Even babies or children will attract situations to give them the learning they need. We may say, 'Well I was born with this condition, how can I be responsible for it?' Remember, our past lives have a part to play in what happens to us. They explain lots of life's mysteries. For example, there may be a reason why a genetic condition is passed on to one child, but not to other members of the family.

"When a problem arises, use it to learn. Ask yourself, 'Why did I attract this problem? Have I ever done the same to anyone? What is the best and most loving way I can handle this? What can I learn from it?'

"You can also help yourself learn more quickly. You could look back on some past problems to see if there was a better way you could have handled them. Could you have been more loving or more effective? Could you have communicated more? Could you have accepted more responsibility? Did you play the victim? Did you worry too much? Did you try to make the other person feel bad or guilty?

"Try to handle problems with as much love as possible. Love yourself as well. You are often unkind to yourself. You easily criticize your own behavior, appearance, etc. If you can't love yourself, you will find it hard to really love anyone else.

"Look at the experiences in your own life. Isn't it wonderful to be able to respond in a loving way, even when it seems that anger is deserved? Don't you feel better when you respond with understanding or make a joke about a difficult situation? Love changes things faster and more permanently than anger ever will. To respond in a loving and understanding way, we need to be centered and balanced. Love, compassion, communication, laughter, generosity of spirit, understanding, fun, and responding from your heart will bring joy to your life and the lives of everyone you meet. Remember that a smile has an effect far beyond the moment it is given.

"Thank you all for listening to me with such patience. I am sure this issue has raised some questions. Please give these ideas time to settle. Listen with your hearts. Sometimes things are rejected because they are so different from what we have believed. Our minds block it and we never give it a chance to reach our hearts to see if it resonates as truth.

"Next week we are going to discuss a subject many of you dismiss as having no importance. We will leave it until then to tell you what it is. We do not wish to start any arguments. Besides, I think you have your hands full with this week's talk," Diana said laughing.

Astrology is an exact science

It can give an accurate guide to your life

You choose the exact moment of your birth

Each planet has an energy that can help you

Your birth connects you to the energy of specific planets

Each zodiac sign has a different quality

The twelve zodiac signs create a balance in the world

· Chapter 19 ·

Astrology

The group of nine sat talking together as they waited for the crowd to seat themselves. Some people delved into the hampers of food that were now becoming a regular sight at these special get-togethers.

They were coming well prepared for the long social evenings that now followed the talks. Almost a seminar in themselves, groups of people gravitated together for discussions. The idea of sharing food had started after the first few weeks, when they began sitting around in circles to chat. Whereas in the beginning it had been just a few sandwiches and a bottle of drink, nowadays amazing creations were coming forth. There was also quite an array of different drinks, including the odd bottle of chilled champagne, in preparation for the warm summer evenings.

They were enjoying themselves and felt they were sharing something far more special than food. The information they heard was not always easy to grasp, but it somehow felt right. Life had certainly not made sense before. There had to be some other picture to life. Now at least they could see a reason for it. And the more they heard, the more it made sense.

It was Carris who stood up this time. "I have been given this week's subject to talk about," she said. "I secretly think the others don't want to be laughed at, because most of you treat this subject as a joke. I am speaking about astrology." She waited. Sure enough, the crowd began to laugh. "You see?" she said, laughing herself, "My colleagues were right.

"Astrology is an exact science,
It can give an accurate guide to your life,
You choose the exact moment of your birth,
Each planet has an energy that can help you,
Your birth connects you to the energy of specific planets,
Each zodiac sign has a different quality,
The twelve zodiac signs create a balance in the world.

"Many of you may be familiar with your zodiac sign. You may know it as a Sun sign. You might know you are a Leo or a Gemini, for example. Some of you may have read the daily forecast for your Sun sign in a magazine. This is a light approach to the subject and a bit of fun. However, it is difficult to be accurate when given in this form. When astrology is understood and used correctly, it can be extremely accurate and helpful.

"Astrology is actually a very exact science, and can provide a detailed picture of your life. It was used as a guide to life in all the ancient civilizations of Earth. The oldest samples of human writing, found in Babylon, were astrological signs.

"A good astrologer can look at where the planets were at your moment of birth and accurately assess your life. This can tell you what you came here to learn, the different abilities you have, and the main events that will happen in your life. They can describe the lessons you have to learn, your ideal work, unresolved issues, and how to use the positive energies of the planets.

"You plan the precise moment of your birth. Although some babies are born earlier or later than anticipated, and some are induced, the time of birth is still as you originally planned it. There is a reason you plan the exact time of your birth. I will explain.

"This idea may be new to you, because we aren't used to thinking that planets have energy. But just as each plant, flower, tree, and mineral on Earth has a different healing energy, so do the planets and zodiac signs.

"You plan out your life to learn certain things, as we have said. Let's say that you wanted to learn about the harmony and sharing involved in relationships. Libra is a sign of balance and relationships. That is why it is represented by a picture of weighing scales, meaning balance. The planet Venus represents love. So, both of these could help you achieve your goal. In order to link with this energy, you would arrange to be born between certain dates in September and October. You are aware of how this works from the spiritual perspective you have before you are born.

"There are twelve zodiac or Sun signs. These divide into the four natural groups: air, fire, earth and water. The total of these create a perfect balance for the world. The air signs are Aquarius, Libra, and Gemini. These represent ideas, logic, intellect, and detachment. The fire signs of Aries, Leo, and Sagittarius cover creative inspiration, enthusiasm, and faith. The water signs are

Pisces, Cancer, and Scorpio. This is the world of emotions and the unseen world of mystery. The earth signs are Virgo, Taurus, and Capricorn and they represent the reliability and stability of the solid ground on which we walk. These signs have to do with common sense and adapting practical skills in any given situation. All the signs also have individual qualities.

"For example, Aries are leaders and project starters. They are full of energy, drive, and a desire to win. Taureans are the rocks of the Earth, resourceful builders and highly dependable. They like down to earth basic food and clothing. Gemini's are good conversationalists and debaters. They often read a lot because they like to know something about every subject. Cancerians have a strong parental caring for people or areas that they feel need their love and protection. The Moon influences Cancer, so physically they often have a round face or body.

"Leo is the sign of the lion and their hair often resembles a lion's mane. Leos are loving, loyal, enjoy attention, and make good leaders. Virgo's are perfectionists, hard workers, and are excellent in jobs requiring attention to detail. They are concerned about their health, so their medicine cabinet is often full. Librans are romantic and harmonious. Being fair and tactful, they make good lawyers and diplomats. Noise, clashing colors and arguments can throw them off balance. Scorpios are passionate, wise, sometimes secretive, and good at any job they are enthusiastic about. Sagittarians are outgoing, positive, and make excellent teachers. They love horses, dogs, and being outside.

"Capricorns are quiet, but ambitious. They climb the ladder of success before anyone notices they are there. Their ambitions may be for their family. They have a wonderful dry sense of humor. Aquarians are the future thinkers. So their interests may include space travel. They relate better to a group rather than to individuals. They usually marry a friend. Pisceans are intuitive, emotional, romantic, and the world's greatest helpers. They are also great spenders. Each sign is associated with a particular part of the body. For example, Leos are associated with the loving heart, Libra the balance of the kidneys and Aries with the thinking of the head.

"There is a great deal more to the subject of astrology, but I hope I have given you some idea of its relevance in our lives.

"Well, that's enough for this evening. It is another beautiful night and I see the food is being brought out already. Enjoy your meal. Next week, same time, same place, we will be talking about our jobs and how to enjoy this part of our life."

Work

Everyone has a wonderful role on Earth

To find your role in life, follow your excitement

When you do what you love, you will do it well

Your abilities are a special part of life

Doing what you love is always in Divine Order

Every necessary task on Earth is enjoyed by someone

Achieving your role in life brings happiness

· Chapter 20 ·

Work

Even though there was still an hour to go before the group was due to arrive, the park was already quite full. People had been coming earlier and earlier each week, taking the opportunity to move around and talk with each other. There was a great harmony and ease between them. Many new friendships had been formed during the past fourteen weeks. Some strong bonds had been created. They were enjoying themselves. People were making up jokes about how they may have met in a past life. There was a lot of laughter about being someone's mother or father before and who still owed money. Someone spoke out and said, "I don't believe in past lives. I didn't last time and I don't this time." This brought more laughter as the joke was passed among the group.

Although the idea of past lives was being joked about, it was uncanny just how many people did feel familiar to each other. As they had not met before, they wondered if some of their jokes may not be all that far from the truth.

Scott came forward to address the crowd. Tall and blond, with smiling eyes, he was another favorite with the ladies in the crowd. It was he who had told them a couple of weeks ago, about how one "caught" a cold. As he stood up to speak, a few people were reminded that they'd had the opportunity to test what he had said. It had worked. Their colds had gone.

"Hello everyone. My name is Scott. This is my third opportunity to speak with you. I feel quite privileged. The gods must be on my side." He turned and grinned at the other eight on the stage. They smiled back. It was obvious to the crowd that they all shared a special bond. They never argued or showed any signs of wanting to be the center of attention. They never seemed perturbed by unexpected circumstances that would cause most people stress, such as when dozens of large birds suddenly landed on the stage all around them. They just smiled and carried on speaking. This must be what they meant by "being balanced."

"I am going to talk about work—the work we chose to do when we planned our life on Earth.

"Everyone has a wonderful role on Earth,
To find your role in life, follow your excitement,
When you do what you love, you will do it well,
Your abilities are a special part of life,
Doing what you love is always in Divine Order,
Every necessary task on Earth is enjoyed by someone,
Achieving your role in life brings happiness.

"As we have said, when you were in the spiritual realms of existence before you were born, you planned what you wanted to achieve in this life. Your purpose here involves some sort of work, so we felt it may help to speak about this area.

"We all have our own ideas about what work is. We may think lying on a beach or relaxing in an office chair isn't really working. Alternately, a laborer shoveling coal in the heat of the day can give us the idea of being hard at work. The truth is, from a spiritual viewpoint, they could all be work, or maybe none of them are. Whatever we came here to do is our work. But it may not be work as we normally think of it.

"You could work very hard at a job for years, but if it was not the job you came here to do, then from a spiritual viewpoint, it is not your work.

"You have to find out what your work is. You may think you are meant to have just one particular job. But this is not necessarily so. You may have planned to do many different jobs. Some of them might only last a minute or two and others may go on for years. Or it may be that you have one task that will last your whole life. The number of jobs we have is not important. As long as we are doing those things that feel right to us at the time, then we are doing the best we can.

"People produce all sorts of different things. But the product is not always obvious. It may be that caring for children or animals, being a friend, giving a cheery smile, sewing, repairing your house, creating a nice garden, cooking, or being positive through hard times could be your spiritual work.

"You may feel that spending the day lying on a beach is irresponsible, especially if there seems to be more important work to do. But it may be your work, at that time. You may be meant to meet someone or be on hand to save a drowning child! You could be having a much needed holiday to help you become more peaceful. These could all be a part of your plan.

"There are signs in your life that show you what you are meant to do. Pay attention to things that interest you. Following what interests you will lead you, step by step, to your heart's dream. You may get an idea while reading a book or watching a television program. A friend may say something that catches your attention.

"We mentioned in our first talk that each of us has a special and unique gift for the world. No one else can do what you are meant to do in the way you do it. You might hope that this will be something special or glamorous. But spiritually, that is not usually what we want. Whatever you planned for your life will interest or excite you. If you planned to be a street sweeper, you would love that idea. You may be thinking, 'Why would anyone plan to sweep streets? I hope I didn't plan that!' If the idea doesn't excite you, that is a sure sign it is not a part of your plan," Scott said, laughing. "However, this job is just as important and special as any other. There are many reasons why people would choose such a job. They may wish to serve others, learn humility, or they may want to keep the place clean! Whatever your job, whether a king, a beggar, or a parent, it is not a sign of how wise or intelligent you are spiritually. Despite what you may think, one job is not easier or better than the other. The type of work you chose was based on what you felt you could do best. Additionally, it often gives you a chance for growth and learning. For example, being disabled in some way may be a wonderful gift you offer, as well as a learning for you. The gift may be to show that, with perseverance and the right attitude, anything can be overcome. At the same time, you could continue your own learning by overcoming this handicap. You may have wanted to learn to remain cheerful, to succeed in business or sport, or even experience how to survive against the odds.

"Whether you know what it is or not, in some way you are giving something to the world that it needs. You may not always see the value of what you do. But there is not one of you here who does not contribute in a special way to the world around you.

"You will always love doing what you came here to do. It will make your heart sing. When you are enthusiastic and animated about something, you will have found the right thing for now. Your special enthusiasm and energy will show in your work. People respond to this and will want what you offer. When you have a quiet moment, ask yourself what you truly enjoy doing. If several different things come to mind, perhaps your work is a combination of them. Or perhaps one is for now and the others later. So, choose the one that excites you most, right now. Producing and achieving your goals will bring happiness.

"There is always something that feels more right to do in each minute than anything else. This even applies to ordinary chores, such as washing dishes and cleaning the car. They are part of life, so there is a place for them. There is a right time to do them. Or it may be that someone else is meant to do them who does find them enjoyable!

"When you do what you love, events will occur that support this. As long as you don't compromise or follow what seems best for your career, then you can benefit from the abundance the universe has to offer. Trust in yourself and your abilities.

"Why don't you live in your heart for one day? Do what you truly want to do in each minute. You may think, 'How wonderful, I will do nothing all day.' Maybe! But that could be the ego or the mind speaking. To find what you really want to do, tune into your heart.

"With a little practice, you will begin to recognize the difference between what your heart is telling you to do and what your mind or ego wants. Your mind is full of what you should or must do. Your ego is concerned about how you appear to others. Your heart is your inner knowing, which will show you your chosen path. You have to get used to tuning into this. Initially, it can help to go somewhere quiet—perhaps the garden.

"A good way to establish if you are where you're meant to be, is to ask yourself, 'If I could be anywhere, doing anything, where would I like to be right now?' If your answer is, 'Right here where I am,' then you know you are following your heart.

"Sometimes we fill our day up with unnecessary jobs we think we *have* to do. We agree to things like committee meetings or making regular visits to someone, because we think it is the *right* thing to do. We try to please people and do things that others expect of us. If we fill our lives in this way, we don't get much time to do things that interest us.

"We all have jobs we are 'going to do,' but haven't yet started or finished them. You may have always wanted to visit a particular place, learn the guitar, or change the cupboard doors. You might not often think of it, but you still have some attention on it. Free up your life and your attention. Make a list of everything in your life that is unfinished. Then either do it, decide you don't want to do it, get rid of it, or get someone else to do it. Freeing up your attention can help you to concentrate better.

"You will need to get used to this way of living. It is a different way to approach things. It is the Golden Way. If you stay aligned to your inner voice and the natural flow of the world, your life will change dramatically. You will always be in the right place, successfully doing what you came here to do. The right people will be around you and you will always get whatever help you need. Your life will be easier and lots more fun. You will feel excited, joyful, and happy.

"That's all for this evening. May your heart sing forever. Allow it to lead the way. We wish you great joy and peace in your life.

"Diana will be speaking to you next week about the many resources that nature offers us.

"Isn't it a beautiful evening? The stars appear to be extra bright. There is also a full Moon, which is always a time of special energy. It helps us to connect to Spirit. Good night everyone."

Earth and Nature

The Earth contains everything we need to live

If we share Earth's resources, there is plenty for all

The Earth maintains a perfect balance of every life form

The planet is entirely self-sustaining

Nature has remedies for all human conditions

Earth's minerals and plants can heal us

The sounds of nature are healing

· CHAPTER 21 ·

Earth and Nature

"Hello again. I know there are new people joining us each week. My name is Diana and I spoke a couple of weeks ago about problems. This time I am going to talk about something especially dear to my heart.

"I have always been very happy and comfortable being out in nature, taking long walks and enjoying all the different seasons and moods she has to offer. Isn't it wonderful to watch a sky turn pink and gold with the setting sun? Or see the power of the ocean waves crashing against the cliffs in a storm? I have learned to appreciate the great beauty even in the smallest and most insignificant things in nature. We know the beauty of a rose, but the perfect patterns in a leaf are also quite beautiful. There is a subtle beauty in nature we can easily miss if we are always in a hurry.

"I am delighted to talk today about the wonderful qualities of Earth and her magnificent world of nature.

"The Earth contains everything we need to live,
If we share Earth's resources, there is plenty for all,
The Earth maintains a perfect balance of every life form,
The planet is entirely self-sustaining,

Nature has remedies for all human conditions,
Earth's minerals and plants can heal us,
The sounds of nature are healing.

"Earth has all the resources it needs to flourish and sustain all life upon it. When nature is left alone to correct itself, it maintains a perfect balance and harmony. When we tamper with this, problems of imbalance occur.

"Contained within Earth's entire system are all the natural tools for mankind to live in an ecologically balanced and healthy way. The various elements found on and in Earth can be used to cure every condition, illness, or disease for every living thing. This includes cures for sick animals, insects, birds, and plants. It does not matter whether our illness is emotional, mental, or physical. Somewhere in nature there is a remedy for everything, whether it is tiredness, a lack of confidence, a mental breakdown, or cancer.

"Although many of our medicines are based on plants and other natural products, the manufacturing process and chemical additives have altered their workability. Lots of nature's healing ingredients are yet to be discovered. While we keep looking for chemical solutions, like medicines and drugs, for our illnesses, we don't look elsewhere. It's only when we realize that artificial methods don't work that we begin to look for other solutions.

"All over the world, healing essences are found in the local water, rocks, plants, earth, minerals, flowers, and trees. Learning about these would make a real difference to our lives. Natural products do not have any side effects when they are taken in the correct quantities. It is possible to intuitively determine the correct amounts to take. This is how it was always done in the past.

"Most people are unaware of the healing power available in nature. We see the beauty of trees, but we miss the potential in the essences of their flowers and seeds. The walnut tree helps you adjust to new changes in your life; beech trees help change feelings of intolerance and arrogance; aspen handles anxiety; pine trees help with feelings of guilt; the olive tree handles extreme physical and mental tiredness; sweet chestnut helps when you reach the end of your endurance; the chestnut bud assists those who keep making the same mistakes in life; willow handles unspoken resentment; elm helps you with feelings of inadequacy; larch helps with expectations of failure, and hornbeam overcomes mental weariness.

"All the different flowers from plants and shrubs on each continent are a part of the healing essences available on Earth. Using those grown locally will give you the greatest benefit. Centaury helps those who allow their good nature to be exploited; chicory handles possessiveness; holly helps erase jealousy and hatred; scleranthus handles mood swings and indecisiveness; the star-of-Bethlehem helps loss, upsets, and sadness; vervain helps with fanatical over-enthusiasm; gorse with hopelessness and despair; mimulus handles fears; crab apple helps those who feel unclean; heather handles self-centeredness; honeysuckle handles our longings for the past; clematis helps the inattentive dreamer; white chestnut quiets a chattering mind; and the cerato flower handles a lack of confidence.

"Healing can also be found in the various minerals of Earth. The oceans contain salt water to heal our wounds. Natural springs give us rock water, which helps release any unbending and rigid views we may have about life. Water contaminated with chemicals, such as fluoride, loses its essential healing qualities.

"The wide variety of crystals and minerals in the ground will handle the broadest spectrum of conditions that affect anything that lives on Earth.

"Natural essences can also help people to come off alcohol, drugs, and other forms of medication. They help with addiction or obsessive behavior. They also help remove toxic poisons built up from alcohol or drugs. The idea is to choose the ones which feel right, to find what works for you.

"The natural essences available today help the body heal itself. However, the underlying reason for these problems would need to be found in order to make sure the situation is not recreated. There are many reasons why people drink excessively, take drugs, or are addicted to sugar. It could be a lack of self-confidence or little joy or sweetness in life.

"Any artificial or chemical medication taken for a period of time can become addictive. Even vitamin tablets, if taken for several months, may tell the body it no longer needs to produce that substance naturally.

"We have spoken about how color can heal us, but we haven't mentioned Earth's natural sounds. Nature provides us with beautiful healing music. A great orchestra of sound can be heard by listening to the wind and the rain. There is one particular sound found throughout nature that has a healing effect. Many people call it OM. It is the sound of thunder and a swarm of bees. It is the sound of an ocean wave crashing onto the shore. It can be heard by holding a large shell to your ear. Many people chant this sound in meditation, to maintain a personal inner balance.

"In addition to nature's sounds, much of our composed music is also healing. Most of us have felt joy from listening to the music we love. Some music makes us feel very relaxed and peaceful. Some music, particularly if heavy, loud, or monotonous, can cause feelings of aggression and an almost drug-like state.

"I have covered just a few of the essences we have available to heal us. There are also other remedies for each condition. Eating fresh, healthy food that is free of drugs, chemicals, and pesticides maintains a healthy body and mind. We've mentioned crystals, minerals, color, sound, positive affirmations, and plant essences. Relaxation techniques can help balance the energy in our bodies. These can alleviate pain and create a healthy body. Massage is very relaxing, particularly when done using healing oils and essences. Touch has a great healing potential. An embrace from a parent can soothe an upset child. Hugging people can actually make them well. And it can be lots of fun. Then, of course, there is love and laughter," Diana said smiling.

"As you can see, the tools are freely available all around us to handle the broadest range of human conditions. Information about natural forms of healing is easy to find.

"Next week we will speak of the wonderful relationship between animals and human beings."

Animals enhance the beauty of life

All species are perfectly balanced in nature

The company of animals can be healing

All animals are capable of communication

Animals have feelings and experience pain and loss

Humans are vegetarians by nature

Animal meat was not intended for human consumption

· CHAPTER 22 ·

Animals

Devora stood up to speak. The people liked her very much. She looked quite angelic. With soft brown eyes and hair that was almost white, she had the sort of translucent skin that stays young and beautiful. They always felt a wonderful love coming from her, which seemed to contain no judgment of them. They had felt it right at the beginning when she had spoken about the power of thought. They knew she was showing them a perfect example of unconditional love.

"This is the last time I will have the privilege of speaking with you," she said, "So I would like to talk about something I hold very dear. That is my deep love for animals." There was a lot of nodding of agreement from the other animal lovers in the audience. They had wondered where animals fitted into the scheme of things. Some people felt uneasy, but they weren't quite sure why.

"Animals enhance the beauty of life,
All species are perfectly balanced in nature,
The company of animals can be healing,
All animals are capable of communication,

Animals have feelings and experience pain and loss,
Humans are vegetarians by nature,
Animal meat was not intended for human consumption.

"Love has long existed between humans and animals. Someone, somewhere, has loved every creature on Earth. And not just our usual pets, such as cats and dogs. People have loved everything from tigers and ducks, to spiders and stick insects. I am sure we all know that animals are capable of great love and companionship. I believe that having a pet can help us live a healthier, happier, and longer life.

"It is even possible to communicate with animals. In fact, many animal healers do just that. But it's possible for anyone to do it. For those of you who feel close to a particular animal, haven't you sometimes felt that you almost speak to each other? Well, perhaps you do." There were some murmurs of agreement from the audience.

"We all have gifts we never use. For instance, we are all capable of telepathy. Haven't we all felt that someone we know would phone or visit, and the person did? Perhaps we have been thinking about someone and they suddenly appear. Or we may have sensed when something was wrong with someone close to us. These are all forms of telepathy. This is also the way we can communicate with animals. Try it! Of course, we need to have a feeling of connection with the animals we want to reach. We also need to feel peaceful within ourselves. It is difficult to use these abilities if we are feeling stressed or upset.

"If we allow it, nature can keep a perfect balance of the animals meant to exist in various parts of the world.

"Perhaps many people don't think of animals as spiritual beings like ourselves, or that they may have similar feelings to us. Generally, we are quite removed from most animals. We are not usually present when animals are born, nor are we involved in the raising of the babies. Nor are we present when they are killed.

"However, we know animals feel pain, because we see their reaction to it. We also see their fear when a hand is raised to hurt them. They are far more aware than we realize. They suffer loss as we do. A cow will cry out for days, as she mourns the loss of her young calf taken away to be killed.

"There is a great upsurge in the number of people becoming vegetarians. Some people choose this diet because of the health benefits. Others don't eat meat because they love animals.

"However, the reason this subject is being addressed today is a spiritual one, to present a viewpoint on how we share the world with all life upon it. This week's talk is a story.

"Once upon a time, there was a land where many people were hungry. They had yet to learn to use the resources that nature offered them. A traveler proposed a solution to the prince. 'You don't have enough animals to provide the milk, eggs, and cheese that your people need. You can change this. First, you must stop people keeping their animals in quarters attached to their homes. Suggest they keep the animals in pens far from the house. Explain this is healthier. People are too fond of the animals. If they're not nearby, the people will forget about them.

"'Then, far away from town, build many barns and animal pens. Take the healthiest males and females of the different breeds. Soon you'll have a lot of produce to feed your people and enough animals to kill them for their meat. Keep their barns warm and artificially lit. If you feed them with chemically treated food, it will stimulate the mating process. As soon as an animal produces offspring, it will mate again. Keep the animals confined indoors. This limits their exercise. They need less feed and remain fat. Keep them out of sight. Your people will be so well fed they won't think about the animals anymore.'"

"Though the prince was not sure about this idea, it was true his people needed more to eat. Someone else had suggested growing gain, but this plan seemed easier. So, he decided to go ahead. The program came into being. The years passed and the people were content.

"Then something odd began to happen. It was barely noticeable at first, just a mention of a neighbor not feeling well. Then a few aches and pains appeared, which people had not had before. Slowly, there were more and more similar stories heard. Strange illnesses began appearing. There was talk of unusual blood conditions and heart problems. Lots of people began experiencing breathing difficulties. There were more deaths than ever before. The problems were not all physical. There were mental disorders as well. Friendly smiles were being replaced with intolerance and arguments. Older people began suffering with memory loss and childish behavior.

"The people were mystified. Finally, they decided it was all the new travelers coming to the town who had brought these unknown sicknesses. Years passed and the sickness increased. People didn't look for reasons any more. Feeling unhappy, or miserable, or sick a lot of the time was just accepted as a part of life.

"Finally, some facts emerged when the farmers gathered together to discuss local farming issues. During the meeting, one old farmer mentioned he never saw any animals anymore. They began chatting about this and realized it was true. They started discussing how the animals had once been such an important part of their lives. Different opinions were voiced about their absence, and other relevant points were raised. One farmer mentioned how much he'd loved working with animals. Other farmers enthusiastically agreed. Someone else mentioned how much fun the children used to have playing with the lambs.

"The meeting came to a close, but in the minds of the farmers, a fire had been lit. A door had been opened which could not be closed.

"Rumors began circulating about how poorly the animals were treated in the breeding compounds. Some people were reluctant to think about this. They were quite happy with their abundant life style and didn't want it changed. But the discontent had started and nothing could stop it. People were reacting. Voices, which had begun softly, now rose in anger and protest. They began demanding changes. This led to more questions and investigations. Finally, they got the truth; that their food supply was of a poor and diseased quality.

"Looking back at it now, they realized they had accepted the original arguments of why they should begin to eat animal flesh, without researching it for themselves. It had seemed reasonable that animals must be a proper source of food for humans. And some had even started to believe that they couldn't live without eating meat.

But now they discovered that the flesh they had been eating was often from animals who were ill with tumors. The animals had been given chemicals to make them fat, more fertile, and to have tastier and better colored flesh. They had been inbred—brother to sister, mother to son—and this had caused genetic mutations.

"Now the people knew the reason for their increased illness. It gave them a great sense of sadness and stupidity. 'We have been ignorant and uncaring,' they said. 'We once shared our homes and loved and cared for these creatures. When one of them was ill we treated it as our own child. We have allowed this abominable act of pain and suffering.' So they went to the barns outside the towns and they tore them down. They took the animals home to be cared for and made well. They swore that nothing like this would ever happen again.

"It had been a harsh lesson. They felt they had lost a great deal. Not only were their bodies sick, but they felt something of their spiritual integrity was lost as well. They knew it would take a long time to correct the damage done. But at least now they were on the road to recovery, both in heart and body.

Slowly the joy of the people increased as they returned to the balance of nature they had once known so well. More and more, they began to use the land to grow a wide range of organic food crops.

"This is the end of this evening's talk," Devora said softly.

With the story over, the people were quiet, their thoughts swirling with dismissal and denial. It was absurd to think this story had some relevance to them.

However, they had a niggling feeling that was hard to deny. They had never checked these things for themselves—just accepted what they had been told. If this was happening in their own community, then they were just as responsible as the people who were mistreating and killing the animals. Ignorance was not a good enough reason for a lack of integrity.

The crowd stayed on for a while after the talk finished. They didn't feel so hungry this evening and a lot of food was left untouched. It was a much quieter and more subdued crowd that packed up to go home.

The quiet didn't last long. The next day the arguments began. At home and at work, all week it raged. Some people were full of rejection and anger, saying they should leave well enough alone. Others demanded they should go and see the conditions in which the animals lived. Heated debates took place, with some people trying to prove they were meant to eat animal flesh, and others with ideas that showed the opposite. "Our teeth are right for it," someone said. Another person said, "Well, just try killing an animal with your teeth and then biting through its hide. But we can do that with raw vegetables." One man said that animals wouldn't exist unless they were meant to be eaten. "Oh yes! And does the same apply to us?" someone else asked. Every imaginable point "for and against" was put forward, discussed, and debated.

The end result, after the confusion had died down, was that a plan of action be put into practice at next week's meeting.

Sleep and Dreams

During sleep, you become your true self

You connect to the realm of Spirit

This connection sustains you throughout your life

Not having enough sleep may prevent this link

As your true self, you have many wonderful abilities

You can travel vast distances during sleep

Dreams can assist you with problems in life

· Chapter 23 ·

Sleep and Dreams

As people entered the park, they were each handed a leaflet. It suggested that a group of people be appointed to form a committee. Their purpose would be to examine conditions involving the various animals that provided food for humans. It suggested that following the investigation, the committee should consider examining all areas involving captive animals. This would include all animals captured or bred for testing the ingredients used in cosmetics and medicines, as well as those providing entertainment in zoos and circuses. The leaflet asked that anyone interested in helping should meet after the talk.

It was a slightly unsettled group who gathered for this week's talk. Many of them still had their attention on the leaflet and the proposed meeting. They were also waiting, with some unease, to see if they were in for any more shocks like the one they had last week. It had stirred up a lot of emotions and arguments. Still, they felt some good had come of it. At least they were going to find out if the same thing was happening in their society. If it were true, they would be better off knowing.

It hadn't been an easy week and it was with relief that they greeted the next topic to be discussed.

"For those who haven't heard me speak before, my name is Dennis. Last time I spoke to you about truth. My subject today is sleeping and dreams.

"During sleep, you become your true self,
You connect to the realm of Spirit,
This connection sustains you throughout your life,
Not having enough sleep may prevent this link,
As your true self, you have many wonderful abilities,
You can travel vast distances during sleep,
Dreams can assist you with problems in life.

"When you go to sleep, it is only your body that is sleeping. You enter another state of awareness. You become your real self. By this, I mean your real self *as a spiritual being*. I know this idea may still seem strange. We are not used to thinking of ourselves in this way.

"There is nothing to fear by thinking of yourself as Spirit. This is a natural state and is quite beautiful. It is one of great power, understanding, freedom, wisdom, harmony and peace. You may not be aware of all the abilities you possess. During your waking hours, your senses are restricted to the five human senses of sight, sound, touch, smell, and taste. But during sleep, you resume your spiritual quality of heightened awareness. In this state, you have many more senses. You are able to see and hear things far beyond what you can when you are in your body. When you are no longer restricted by normal eyesight, you can see everything with a 360-degree view.

"As your true self, you also have many abilities that have been learned in previous lifetimes. However, you will not be aware of most of them because they aren't needed as part of your current life. I will explain. Imagine that you have previously been a musician, a doctor, a parent, and a tradesman. You have learned the many skills involved in these roles. This lifetime you have decided to concentrate on learning discipline and devotion. You are going to enter a holy order to achieve this. You can see that your former skills would not be needed and would even be a distraction to your purpose. You would therefore choose not to have them as part of your life. So, you see, you are far more able than you realize.

"You use this period of sleep for several purposes. While asleep, you reestablish your energy connection to the spiritual world. It is sort of like recharging your batteries. In your life, if you usually follow your intuition and do what feels right, then you maintain your connection to a spiritual source of energy. However, if you usually do what society or other people say you should do, or must do, you become disconnected from this spiritual energy. This means you step out of the natural flow of the universe. This drains the energy in your body and makes you feel tired. Other things can also drain your energy. Excessive use of alcohol, drugs, or a lack of sleep also prevent this connection and recharging taking place. This can be very harmful to your well-being.

"Another thing you do while your body sleeps is review the day's activities. Using your higher spiritual awareness, you sort things out in your mind. You look at any fears you may have that are stopping you from doing things that will benefit you. You try to get a clearer picture of the best way to resolve any problems you have. Sometimes, you wake up with a much clearer understanding. Though you may not remember you have resolved a problem, you might suddenly start to handle things differently. It is possible to wake up with the entire solution to a problem.

"Have you ever woken up with a feeling of only being half there? This can happen when you are suddenly awakened. This occurs because you are suddenly pulled back from your spiritual dimension of existence.

"Dreams can be beneficial. Sometimes they are just a mix-up of things that don't make any sense. But, at other times, they can help you recall that you solved a problem while you were asleep. If something is recorded in a dream, you are more likely to remember the solutions you worked out.

"Before I close this evening, here is something else for you to think about. In your natural state, you are able to travel anywhere. It is possible that sometimes what you thought was a dream could have been an actual visit you made somewhere. You may have been off chatting to friends in some distant exotic location! So you see, you might be much more traveled than you think," he said smiling.

"Next week's talk might be of interest. We will be covering the subject of angels and God. I know there are people here from different faiths who will use a different word to mean the 'source of creation.' It is the overall understanding that we will be looking at and not a specific faith.

"I wonder where you will be off to tonight in your sleep? Perhaps we will all join up for a drink," he said laughing. "Anything is possible!"

He smiled at them, and once again they had a feeling of understanding something beyond the spoken words. This had often happened during these talks. It was difficult to define, but in that moment you knew that a great truth was only a whisper away.

"I look forward to seeing you next Sunday." Still smiling, he bowed to them, as he moved to the side of the stage to help Devora put the scrolls out.

God and Angels

God is the Consciousness that exists in everything

Every living thing is a part of that Consciousness

The world is co-created

There are many dimensions of existence

Life exists in every dimension

No one religion or philosophy has all the truth

Everyone has a Guardian Angel

· CHAPTER 24 ·

God and Angels

It was Michael who stood up to speak this evening. The people had given nicknames to some of the speakers. Michael had been dubbed "the ageless one." Many in the crowd had guessed he would be the one covering this week's subject. They weren't sure why. It could have been that special quality of caring he seemed to have that one tends to associate with God and angels. When they saw they were correct, they started laughing. They began to joke with each other, saying, "At long last, our intuition is working. And it's only taken us seventeen weeks!"

"We are drawing near the end of our talks," Michael said. With that, everyone began talking at once. He stood quietly allowing them to adjust to the idea. It was a good few minutes before they settled. "We understand some of you may feel a sense of loss about this, but I wish to explain something. There is more to these events than just the information you have been receiving. It is also an awakening. A door has been unlocked, which will allow you to see beyond what you have previously known. You will have more questions about life, but you will no longer need us. You will discover the answers are both within you and all around you. It will be an exciting and rewarding journey.

"These evenings have been a great joining of hearts and minds—and food," he said smiling. "You have formed new friendships. You have looked at new perspectives on life. You have shared in the ups and downs—and the arguments," he said grinning. "We hope you feel you have grown together in a new understanding. We have also experienced the harmony and joy of being here with you. We have watched the love grow between you. It has shown us that what has taken place here can happen everywhere. Don't let go of what you have felt here. Hold it in your hearts and take it into your environments. When you are sure within yourself of these new ideas, perhaps you will wish to share them with others. Don't worry if people laugh or think you are a little mad. Didn't you think we were mad in the beginning? You probably still do," Michael said laughing. "It is not important what others think; the importance lies in the richness and joy of discovery.

"No talks about life would be complete without going into the subject of God. I realize that some of you use a different word than God for the source of creation. I ask your forgiveness, but there are many names used for this sacred concept, and we had to choose one.

"This is another tricky area; one that has caused many arguments—and many wars. As you see, we have left it to near the end, so we can make a run for it if necessary!" The people laughed. "So I shall be brave and tell you how we see it.

"God is the Consciousness that exists in everything,
Every living thing is a part of that Consciousness,
The world is co-created,
There are many dimensions of existence,
Life exists in every dimension,
No one religion or philosophy has all the truth,
Everyone has a Guardian Angel.

"Some teachings in our culture and religions refer to a God of judgment. Most speak of the necessity of following a specific path, believing theirs to be the only path of truth. Some tell us that if we leave this path, we will become lost souls. Although, we may not realize it, this can make us fearful. Perhaps even of God. We may no longer feel free to search for truth in other areas of life. Nothing works well that is enforced by fear. Because our spiritual goal is to love, eventually we will leave anything that restricts this.

"There is a value in encouraging people to live in a caring manner, but it works best when done in a positive way. Fear stops us from truly loving. For example, if you are afraid of the sea, you will not enjoy sailing. If you find technical things complicated, you will find there is some fear present. If you are afraid, even a little, of snakes or spiders, you probably won't want one as a pet," he said smiling.

"We believe each of you is immortal, and has eternal and everlasting life, regardless of the path you follow. However, to find true peace within yourself requires a commitment on your part. This is a path. It begins the day you decide to seek truth. If your desire is genuine, and your intent is pure, from that moment you will be led to the answers that you seek, even if you do not yet know what they are.

"We are going to suggest a different way to think about God. Our answer is simple. It is not hidden in ancient manuscripts or restricted to any one sect or religion. It is not necessary to go to a place of worship, or to sit on a mountaintop in deep meditation, although this may be comforting and beneficial. The answer is available to anyone who can look beyond his or her existing beliefs.

"Our world and what lies beyond it is a most magnificent creation. How it came about has been a source of wonder throughout time. Many people believe the Creator to be a specific person located in a higher place of existence. Our own view of creation is that the source of life is a combination of everything that exists. In other words, we are all the Consciousness of Creation. God is both within and is each one of you.

"But to fully understand our precious gift of life, we believe that you each need to seek the truth within. When and if you wish to, you will find your own answer—within yourself. It comes when you have a desire to know the real truth about life. It is then that you are ready to move beyond the limited ideas of your world. When you are ready to find yourself, we believe you will find God.

"When you discover the real you, you will find a wonderful person who is loving, peaceful, and joyful. Your inner light shines most radiantly. That inner light is part of a great universe of light.

"Beyond what we can see, other forms of life also exist on Earth. These exist in a different vibration or energy, which is too fast for our human eyes to see. But, with our spiritual eyes we can see these other dimensions and the people in them.

"Life also exists on other planets. Some planets have people on them. We tend to assume that if there were life on other planets, the people would be the same as us. However, because of the different bodies or difference in energy vibration, they do not require the same conditions of existence we do. So, they would not necessarily need oxygen or food.

"Most of us cannot see in these other dimensions of existence. But there are some people who can see things we can't. We usually call this a sign of insanity. We would think someone was insane if they pointed to an empty chair and said to us, 'Don't sit in that chair, there is someone already in it.' If they went on saying it, they would probably be locked away. But, what if there really was someone sitting in the chair? Someone that we could not see, but they could? What if it was a ghost, someone who had died and is still around? Ghosts have spiritual bodies. You also have one. You use it when you are sleeping.

"So, is the person insane? Or is he or she just able to see something that we cannot? Perhaps a lot of the people in insane asylums are there only because they can see things that society is unwilling to accept as possible. Perhaps if we had more of an understanding of these other dimensions, we could help people who had simply become aware of another level of existence.

"Angels are also part of the—normally unseen—life that exists in other dimensions. Some of you may believe, or perhaps hope, that you have a Guardian Angel. Well, we believe everyone has a Guardian Angel. They help you quite a lot without you ever realizing it.

They help and guide you with the learning you arranged in this life. You do not have to be religious to have an angel. Just as you make plans before your birth with the people involved in your life, you also make plans with a Guardian Angel. You also have angels that help with everyday things. For example, they can assist you to find things you have lost. They listen to your prayers and help when they can. They also help rearrange plans that have been broken by other people not keeping to their agreements, so that you still gain the opportunities you wanted. They can help fix situations that occur when you did not listen to your inner voice and things went a little astray. They are kept quite busy," Michael said smiling. The people began joking with each other, as they recalled the things in their lives that had "gone a little astray!"

Michael waited, enjoying the joke with them.

"I move on from the idea of angels, and ask you what about the fairies?" He stopped, waiting for the reaction. The people began laughing again. "Perhaps you have heard stories of people seeing fairies. Have you ever wondered if they may be true? That perhaps fairies do exist in other dimensions around us? Many people feel comfortable believing in a God they can't see, but dismiss other unseen areas. Actually, aside from fairies and different types of angels, there are also gnomes—the real garden variety—and elves and pixies. So now you can think I am really crazy." There were more smiles and nods in the crowd.

"You may find that if you were not afraid that someone would laugh at you, you could be quite open to the idea that fairies and angels exist. Your life would be the richer for including these beautiful, gentle creatures into your world.

"You don't hear about it often, for understandable reasons, but many people can see them and even talk with them. You could also do that. You would need to become very positive and gentle, and attune yourselves to this softer vibration of life. But you could do it. Fairies are not very comfortable with negative vibrations.

"Well, I am off to talk with the fairies," Michael said laughing. "We will see you next week when Anthony will be talking about how to live a happy life."

How to Live a Happy Life

Be yourself

Have fun and enjoy life

Do things that interest and excite you

Trust in the process of Divine Order

Make your choices from your inner knowing

Be compassionate, loving, and tolerant

Don't live according to what others expect

· CHAPTER 25 ·

How to Live a Happy Life

The man who came forward to speak had a fan club in the crowd. Perhaps it was the boyish smile, or his lovely silver hair, that appealed to the females in the crowd. His good looks and physique had acquired him the title "Apollo," an ancient Greek god known for his handsome appearance. Some people felt Anthony was the leader of the group, perhaps because he had given them the first message. However, they now realized that there was no leader in this group. All nine of its members had spoken extremely well, and, it had seemed, with equal authority. Some people realized their idea that there had to be a leader was just an old belief pattern. The people were now beginning to put into practice many of the things they had learned over the last few months.

"We have reached the last in our series of talks," Anthony said.There was a murmur through the crowd. "We feel it is appropriate as we close, to mention some of the points that are most relevant in living the Golden Way.

"Be yourself,
Have fun and enjoy life,
Do things that interest and excite you,
Trust in the process of Divine Order,
Make your choices from your inner knowing,
Be compassionate, loving, and tolerant,
Don't live according to what others expect.

"You have a choice in life. You can live a rewarding, useful, and happy life. But to achieve it, you will need to become your true self. You can work out how much you are truly being yourself. You will have to be honest. If you answer 'Yes' to any of the following questions, some changes are needed to truly live the Golden Way.

Do you put up barriers to stop being hurt?
Do you sometimes act falsely with people?
Do you find yourself copying what other people do?
Do you think if people really knew you, they wouldn't like you?
Do you seek approval before doing anything?
Are you playing out life hiding behind a role?
Do you feel you are not clever enough to join in conversations?
Are you being carried along by life's events?
Do you feel you can't exist without a particular person?

"You can also check whether you are making choices by intuition, or by doing what your mind and ego is telling you. Are any of your actions based on the following?

a) What you think you should do?
b) How much money it will make?
c) Trying to make other people like or love you?
d) Trying to impress with your wisdom?
e) Because you are afraid?

"If you answered, 'Yes,' to any of these, maybe you could listen more to your intuition. Find the courage to trust it. It will truly help you find what you seek.

"I am going to mention life's 'mirror' again." He turned to grin at Diana. "They won't forget the mirror," he said laughing. "Life is a great reflection. This means the people you attract into your life will be similar to you. If you are truly loving, generous, and tolerant, most people around you will be the same.

"If you are critical, unloving, impatient, a bully, rude, greedy, or egotistical, then those are the types of people you will mainly find in your life. If you lack integrity, deceive people, make others less confident, or even talk too much, you need to experience this yourself, to see you are doing it.

"Someone can appear to be generous, but it may not be real generosity. Perhaps they can't be responsible for owning things. They might give things to people because they want to be liked.

"When you trust enough to 'let go' and just be yourself, the people who respond to you will be those who are genuinely drawn to who you truly are.

"Our true nature is one of love. Nonloving behavior is not natural. Sometimes we act a certain way for so long we forget we aren't really like that. We act out our old patterns of behavior and never stop to see how we truly are.

"It is easy to change. Take notice of your thoughts and actions. If you find they are negative, change them. Thoughts are powerful. Saying, 'I can't do that,' can be creating a future where you really 'won't be able to do it.' Adding the words 'up until now' to a negative statement will change it to a more positive one.

"It takes a little courage to be honest with yourself. If you see something that needs changing, change it. Be determined.

"Once you decide to become yourself, your next step is to stay there. Don't be drawn back into your old patterns. Not for any reason. You don't have to impress anyone by behaving in a way that isn't truly you. Let the beautiful 'you' emerge.

"Become more tolerant of others and their ideas. If you feel compelled to judge or criticize, change it to a feeling of love. If you knew the circumstances behind people's actions, you would probably be more understanding. You would be less likely to judge. For example, if you knew someone who was being impatient with you just had some terrible news, you'd probably be more tolerant, wouldn't you?

"There is a natural order and flow to life. If you fight it, life can seem to be a never-ending uphill struggle. If you flow with it, life is interesting and enjoyable. Your intuition is part of that flow. It shows you, through your feelings of interest and excitement, the things that are exactly right for you. If you listen, it will always guide you to your highest good. The universe is rich and abundant. When you move in the flow of life, you will receive everything you need to live joyfully. What you receive will be what you are 'truly choosing at every level of learning.' Perhaps not always what you think should happen," he said grinning.

"Earlier on in our talks, Dennis wondered if you would like to continue meeting in the park to share your views after we have gone. If you are interested in this idea, would you please raise your hands?" Hundreds of hands went up, way across the park.

"Well, that is certainly clear," he said laughing. "It is an exciting journey to be sharing together. So, do you want to meet at the same time, same day, and same place? Is everyone in agreement with that?"

There was a resounding, "Yes," from the audience. Everyone started laughing and clapping. Michael laughed also. "Can this really be the reserved group of people who, just a few months ago, believed us to be mad? I think I will leave that alone, before all the jokes start. I am going to hand you over now to Talia, who would like to give you some parting thoughts.

"For myself, I would like to say the time we have spent together has been a great joy for me. With all my heart, I wish you great happiness on the special journey that lies ahead. I know you can make a real difference to your own lives and to the world.

"As you know, we intend to continue with our talks in other places and take this understanding of life to those who desire it.

"We will meet again one day, my friends. Somewhere.

"For the world to change, we must first change ourselves.

For peace and harmony to exist in the world—it must first exist within us.

Allowing the Golden Way to unfold in your heart will make your dreams come true.

A Bridge

Trust in yourself and your abilities

Be true to yourself in all you do

Give yourself time for peace and self-growth

Let your heart love unconditionally

Understand that you create your world

Have faith and trust in the higher picture

Follow what makes your heart sing—
without hesitation

· Chapter 26 ·

A Bridge

Talia came to the front of the platform, still smiling from the enthusiastic response of the audience. She stood calmly, her fair hair moving gently in the breeze, as it had been the first time they saw her. Her beautiful eyes showed the love she felt for them all. She looked more radiant than ever, perhaps because she knew the group had achieved what they set out to do. They had made a difference.

She had held a special place in their hearts since she had spoken to them on that first day. It seemed so long ago now; so much had changed. They knew they were not the same as before. They behaved differently with people. They cared much more, not just for families and friends, but for everyone. They liked who they had become. They liked themselves.

"From the points Anthony has just mentioned, you may feel there are still some changes you would like to make in your life. Here are some steps I found valuable to me.

"Trust in yourself and your abilities,
Be true to yourself in all you do,

Give yourself time for peace and self-growth,
Let your heart love unconditionally,
Understand that you create your world,
Have faith and trust in the higher picture,
Follow what makes your heart sing—without hesitation.

"As Anthony told you, we are to move on this week. We intend to take our message to other people. Michael mentioned that you may feel a loss about us leaving. But there is no excuse for anyone getting a cold from this," she smiled.

"For us, these five months have gone by quickly. To you, perhaps they have seemed to take forever," she said with her infectious laugh. "Don't be concerned if any of you still feel a bit confused. It may take a little while to digest all we have said. This is a normal reaction when one is uprooted from deeply held beliefs. Be patient and allow time for any confusion to pass. In its place, there will be new peace and contentment. As we told you earlier, we do not want you to blindly accept what we have said. We are only suggesting that you try looking at life from this different perspective. Give yourself a chance to see if these principles are correct.

"We have shared a special journey together. But it is the journey, and not us, that is special. We had some information to share and now you have it. You don't need us any more. Further clarity will come with each new day, as you begin to view events in your life from a new perspective. Begin by following those things we have suggested today. As you understand more about the higher picture to life, we believe you will see the ideas we have been discussing will work for you. When they are applied, life definitely becomes more enjoyable. We hope they will become an accepted part of society and the way people look at life.

"We mentioned at the start of our talks that from our early childhood we had felt we had a message to share. We understand some of you may be curious as to how this came about. We don't want you to have to speculate on this after we have gone. You will be busy enough with your exciting new lives," she said smiling.

"It began when we were very young. Most of us were just 8 to 10 years old. I had attended a holy service with my parents. Afterward, I noticed a wonderful golden glow coming from the large crystal on the altar. We had all heard our parents speak of this crystal. It had apparently been sitting there for as long as anyone could remember. A legend spoke of it coming from a great civilization of peace, which had existed many thousands of years ago. It was quite beautiful and many of the children felt it was very special.

"What followed may sound strange to you, as it would to most people. As I looked at the crystal, it began telepathically speaking to me. Later it was to talk to all of us. It communicated to us in thoughts, but we could all hear it clearly. We were told we were to help with a change coming to Earth. It said it had information to give to us that would help create a better world. It somehow transmitted this information to us. As children, we didn't understand the words, but what it was saying felt right to us. We knew this was what we were meant to do with our lives. The crystal relayed to us that we need not concern ourselves with these things for some years. When we became adults, we would know what to do. This turned out to be true. As we grew older, we each became aware that we were meant to speak to people and deliver the messages we had been given. We are doing this.

"We have all so enjoyed being here with you. It has been a wonderful experience for us. We are grateful to you for listening and thank you for your patience. We know it hasn't always been easy. We have certainly come up with some strange ideas," she said smiling. "We hope it has helped you with your life journey and it will make the path ahead clearer for you. We know that with wisdom and determination, you can create a joyful place to live.

"If you choose to take the path we have shown you, your life will become more wonderful than you can imagine. Understanding about life brings great happiness and serenity. Our inner being comes alive with a magical quality that cannot be explained in words. Beyond the apparency of what seems to be, beyond the days and years, we begin to exist in one moment of sheer joy.

"We believe the things we have shared can be a new beginning for you. Perhaps it will be the beginning of a new world. We call it the Golden Way."

We love you all unconditionally.

It started slowly at first. Just a murmur through the crowd. Then, spontaneously, everyone was on their feet, clapping and cheering. With love and gratitude, the crowd, in One Voice, One Breath, One Mind and

One Heart, acknowledged this special group of nine who had visited their lives and changed them forever.

The nine stood quietly, smiling. Then, bowing their heads in thanks, they began to leave the stage.

The clapping could still be heard, filling the air with joyous harmony, as the nine walked quietly from the park and disappeared!

Not the end, but a new beginning . . .

Live the Golden Way

See the beauty that is all around you.
Follow your intuition—your heart, your passion.
Realize you are worthwhile and valuable.
Laugh more often.
Do things you enjoy—treat yourself.
Fill your life with the relaxing and happy music you love.
Help others and share with them—small gestures can change lives, including yours.
Watch light-hearted films.
Avoid violent or valueless programs.
Wear loose clothes, natural fabrics, and light colors.
Get your priorities right.
Remind yourself you are valuable.
Do some fun exercise.
Do not judge or criticize people.
Avoid gossip.
Make money instead of debts.
Wear colors and styles that feel right and suit you.
Love yourself—be your own best friend.
Wherever you go, take the calm and silence within you.

Life is a natural high without the use of alcohol and drugs.
Decide if you need newspapers, radio, or TV news in your life.
Smile a lot—it's catching.
Walk in nature.
Have a job you love (yes, you can).
Look at waterfalls and oceans.
Organize the paperwork (while listening to lovely music).
Have a pet you love.
Have bright, cheery friends.
Sell or give away everything in your life you don't use, don't like, or don't enjoy.
Be positive about everything. Yes, everything.
Ask for help whenever you need it.
Let go of the idea that you need things.
Praise people.
Watch lots of stars and sunsets.
Give and receive lots of hugs.
Make a special box or place to cheer you up and remind you how special you are. Put in cards, letters, articles, poems, small gifts, messages, pictures, certificates, commendations, successes, and your own inspired thoughts.
Send cheerful, positive, loving letters.
Be responsible for your thoughts and actions.
Walk with friends.
Make positive affirmations.
Play with animals.
Discover the natural ways to heal yourself.
Meditate in stillness.

Give and receive massages.
Create a wish list.
Learn an exciting new skill.
Let go of ideas about how young or how old you are.
Go somewhere you always wanted to go.
Meet or write to people who inspire you.
Set a wonderful example (children and others copy our actions).
Play the wonderful game of life.
Use crystals.
Be the person you want to be.
Make your home clutter and chaos free (sell, swap, give, or throw things away).
Pay off your debts.
Save 10 percent of your income.
Avoid negative people and those you don't like.
Fill your life with positive people, thoughts, reading, and listening.
Write "thank you notes" and letters commending people who have done a good job.
Free up your life. Make a list of everything in your life that is incomplete. Then either do it, decide you don't want to, or get someone to do it for you.
Don't fill your mind with endless thoughts and worry.
Invest quality time with loved ones.
Find the best in everyone.
Soak in lovely bubble baths.
Send out Light, prayer, good thoughts, and love.
Live in a home, town, and country you love.
If you want a car—get one you love.

Exchange services with people (barter).
Have fun—life is joyful.
Leave any soul-destroying job or relationship.
Stand tall and straight.
Forgive quickly and freely, yourself as well.
Leave the chores you dislike for someone who loves them.
When you drive, listen to tapes to entertain, inspire, or educate.
Look at all the "right" things people do.
Write down five things you are grateful for each morning—read them.
Let go of guilty feelings. If it feels right, make amends.
Do what you do well.
Love people.
Love life.
Decide you can.

Around the Home

Lovingly create your dream home, even if renting.
Have white or pastel colored candles lit.
Use essences and essential oils.
Have quiet times.
Have a well lit home—sunlight if possible.
Make beautiful curtains and covers.
Have light colored or natural furniture.
Paint or wallpaper in colors you love.
Build an indoor waterfall.
Avoid dark or clashing colors and dark furniture.
Keep your environment in order.
Keep the house and car clean.
Clean and open your windows to the world.
Enjoy lots of indoor plants or perfumed flowers.
Create a garden, make your own compost.
Keep the lawn mowed and the garden tidy.
Use non-toxic house paint, furniture, and furnishings.
Avoid chemical garden fertilizer and pest control methods.

Natural Health

Get lots of sunlight, without sunburn.
Drink lots of good quality water.
Eat delicious fresh, light foods in small quantities.
Live a chemical, drug, and pesticide-free life.
Find out the natural ways to heal yourself and your body.
Make your own fruit and vegetable juices.
Avoid inhaling toxic fumes from paints, petroleum cleaners, etc.
Locate an excellent natural health practitioner to use and recommend.
Grow your own organic vegetables.
Dry your own fruit.
Use natural healing herbs and vitamins.
Use natural fabrics and products, including soap, shampoo, and toothpaste.
Eat fresh organic vegetables and salad.
Use natural make-up or none.

Affirmations

I am perfect just the way I am.
I love everyone, everywhere, and they all love me.
I am always in the right place at the right time, doing the right thing.
I am invincible.
I am in perfect health.
I have everything I need to be comfortable.
I am positive in everything I say, think and do.
I learn quickly.
I am peaceful and calm.
My inner guidance leads me to perfect situations.
I have faith and trust in the process of life.
I am open to the abundance of the universe.
I always have enough energy to do everything I want.
I release everything that is holding me back.
I always listen to my intuition.
I am patient and tolerant.
My world is filled with love, joy, beauty, peace, and comfort, always.
I am perfectly guided.
I accept differences in others.

There are endless ways of doing things and seeing things.
I love life and life loves me.
I allow the realities of others to pass without reaction.
I move forward with love in my heart.
The world is perfect.
I am at peace.
I live in harmony with the whole world.
The world is full of lovely people.
I am completely positive.
There is nothing stronger than I am.
I control my life and my destiny.
I judge or criticize no one.
I follow my inner guidance.
I am always being shown the next right move.
I am supported in hundreds of ways.
I choose the changes in my life.
I teach only love.
I am willing to see things differently.
I act from inspiration.
I deserve love, happiness, and abundance.

Glossary

Astral Plane: A nonphysical plane or level of existence close to the Earth. It looks similar to Earth.

Atlantis: An ancient civilization that sank in the Atlantic Ocean long ago.

Being: You. The person, soul, spirit.

Conditional Love: Love that is given only if certain conditions are met.

Crystal: A natural element found on Earth that has healing properties.

Dimension: Refers to a level of existence. There are many dimensions.

Divine Order: "In the flow." The natural flow and order of the world, where everything happening is the very best for the learning and growth of all concerned.

God: The combined Consciousness of the universe.

Golden Way: A spiritual way of living.

Incarnation: Living a life in a physical body.

Level: See *dimension*.

Physical Body: A human body. Used for identity during an incarnation.

Physical World: Everything we can see.

Plane: See *dimension*.

Spirit: The energy of all life.

Spiritual Being: The person.

Third dimension: Everything that can be seen in the physical world.

Unconditional Love: The complete acceptance of others just as they are. Love without expecting anything in return.

Vibration: A frequency of energy (vibes).

Zodiac: The path of the major planets and the Moon in a circular area around the Sun.

Zodiac sign: Refers to one of the twelve signs: Aries, Taurus, Gemini, Cancer, Leo, Virgo, Libra, Scorpio, Sagittarius, Capricorn, Aquarius, and Pisces.

Recommended Reading

Louise Hay, *You Can Heal Your Life.* Los Angeles: Hay House, 1984. This bestseller teaches you how to love yourself. It also provides a comprehensive list of the mental thought patterns that cause most of our physical discomfort, illness, and disease.

Michael J. Roads, *Talking with Nature*. Los Angeles: H. J. Kramer, 1987. A remarkable story of one man's communication with nature.

Mechthild Scheffer, *Bach Flower Therapy*. London: Thorsons/HarperCollins, 1986. An easily followed, self-diagnostic approach to using nature's plants and flowers for healing.

Recommended Music

The people on this list are gifted musicians. You may not be able to obtain their music easily. You may want to contact them.

Sally Brown
Trafalgar Cottage
Trethillick
Padstow
Cornwall. PL28 8HJ
United Kingdom

Singer and songwriter. Vocal and instrumental music cassettes and CD's. Write for details.

John Christian
2 Saint Katherine's Cottage
Green Field Lane
Ickleford
Hertfordshire. SG6 1XS
United Kingdom

Vocal music cassettes and CD's. He leads treks to Nepal. Please write for details.

Chris James
Sounds Wonderful Pty., Ltd.
P. O. Box 160
Warrandyte
Victoria 3113
Australia

Website: www.chrisjames.net
Email: cjames@chrisjames.net

Vocal music cassettes and CD's. Effective, fun workshops where you can learn singing, voice training, or teaching. Write or contact his website for details.

Born in Australia, Sandy Stevenson moved to England in 1965, beginning a search for a greater spiritual understanding of life.

Many personal experiences during the past 35 years have led her to a deeper insight into the purpose of life. Sandy, along with many others, believes that when we look at life from a particular viewpoint, we see a wonderful plan that is designed to teach us greater love, wisdom, and compassion.

During the past 10 years, Sandy has given workshops in the UK, Australia, New Zealand, Zimbabwe, Hong Kong, and many countries in Europe. Her workshops are presented in a humorous and easily understood way. They show life as a wonderful journey of enlightenment that brings peace, harmony, and joy. Above all, Sandy encourages people to trust in themselves and to follow their dream.